The Heart of the Prophetic

THE [HEART] OF THE PROPHETIC

IVAN ROMAN

ENDORSEMENTS

Rarely do I get excited about a "new" prophetic book, because most of them lack "new." Ivan Roman's new book is Phenomenal! Turn off your smart phone, sit down for two hours, and strap yourself in for a mindset-changing book. Even if you have been a Charismatic for years, you will find this book filled with surprising gems.

DR. JONATHAN WELTON
Welton Academy Supernatural Bible School
Best-selling author of *School of the Seers*
www.weltonacademy.com

Ivan Roman is a prophetic teacher, a good prophetic teacher, and his book *The Heart of the Prophetic* captures this. There is a new generation of leaders talking about walking out the prophetic ministry and lifestyle journey, and Ivan is a voice you need to listen to. Ivan combines excellent theological perspective with gripping stories, and you will grow as you take part this great resource.

SHAWN BOLZ
Author of *Translating God, Keys to Heaven's Economy, Growing Up With God*
www.bolzministries.com

Ivan is a pursuer of God and the things of God. Since I first met him at BSSM, I have been impressed with this characteristic. This book is an expression of that and it invites the reader into that journey for themselves. *The Heart of the prophetic* is great teaching on the prophetic, but it is more than that, as it is really equipping the believer with a life of hearing God, leading and ministering out of that. I know the man and I know his God, and I commend this man to you. I invite you to hear God more as a result of this helpful practical and inspiring book.

PAUL MANWARING
Bethel Church, Redding CA

I highly recommend my good friend Ivan Roman's new book called *The Heart of the Prophetic*. This is more then a good read! It's a heavenly blueprint to moving in greater realms of intimacy and breakthrough in the things of God. In this book you will learn how to soar to new heights in the realm of The prophetic as well as hearing God's voice. Be inspired as you read and discover the Fathers love and heart for your life which will in turn unlock your identity and launch you into your destiny.

JERAME and MIRANDA NELSON
Living At His Feet Ministries
Author of *Burning Ones: Calling Forth a Generation of Dread Champions, Encountering Angels,* and *Manifesting God's Love Through Signs, Wonders, and Miracles: Discovering the Keys of the Kingdom*

I have known Ivan Roman and his prophetic journey for many years and have personally seen his accurate prophetic gifting and character touch countless lives. I know his new book on *The Heart of the Prophetic* will equip and ready you to live a true prophetic lifestyle and release the word and heart of God.

TODD BENTLEY
Fresh Fire USA
Author of *The Reality of the Supernatural World, Journey into the Miraculous,* and *Christ's Healing Touch Vol. 1*

I have known Ivan Roman as a friend and minister for many years, and have seen a man of great honor and truth. His new book *The Heart of the Prophetic* is a must read for anyone desiring inspirational truth and revelational teaching. Ivan has operated in the prophetic gift for many years, and has taken his experience and the Word of God and molded them together in a practical and revelational way. He truly carries a prophetic gift for "such a time as this," and I encourage anyone interested and/or ministrering in the prophetic to read this book.

BRENT BORTHWICK
President/Founder of Windword Ministries
Senior Leader of Windword Churches

DEDICATION

Writing a book is not a one person job. The time and people it takes to see a book from start to finish is more than most realize.

I want to first and foremost thank my beautiful wife Erica. It's hard enough to put up with me, let alone when I'm consumed with a project from God. Erica you are my constant support and friend.

To my three boys, Isaiah, Aren and Ezra. My prayer is that you would understand the heart of our Father toward each of you, and walk in intimate friendship with Him.

To Angela Hughes for editing, transcribing and encouragement along the way.

I would also like to thank Dr. Jonathan Welton for blazing a trail with New Covenant teaching. The church is better off because of you.

Lastly, I would like to thank Empowered Life Church for believing in me. You guys rock!

TABLE OF CONTENTS

INTRODUCTION

I often wonder what it would be like to walk with Jesus on the shores of the Sea of Galilee. I could have witnessed Him performing miracles, witnessed the unrecorded events in scripture, witnessed how He treated people, and maybe the tone in which he spoke to people. We read scriptures and can easily misinterpret them because of our experience, or our filter of theology. I am convinced that Jesus was more than a miracle worker, or theologian. Jesus being fully God and fully man is the embodiment of love itself. The bible doesn't say only that God loves, but that God is love. The more I walk with Jesus, the more I am convinced of His goodness and love.

Religion has not done the greatest job revealing Christ from the scriptures. Many in the church have settled for a life less than Christ has purchased for us at the Cross. For this reason, I believe the Father is rising up a people that will rightly represent Him on the earth. He is rising up a prophetic people that carry not only the gifts of the Spirit that break the chains of discouragement, but a people that model the very heart of the Father and a Christ like life.

Historically, we have seen many moves of God come and go. Very often the personalities of the catalysts are larger than life, and many of the moves of God have ended because of some sort of compromise in the life of the minister. A desire for the power of God without knowing the person of God will always lead us into the sin of pride. This phenomenon has caused people to not pursue walking in the fullness of the normal Christian life.

The scripture teaches us that "faith works through love" Galatians 5:6. Those who love the most will not only see the greatest faith released on the earth, but also the greatest long lasting fruit.

"In this is my Father glorified that you bear much fruit." John 15:8NIV

I am convinced that when the love of God is allowed to flow through our hearts by the Holy Spirit, we will see a generation represent Christ to the world with love, truth and grace. We have yet to see a generation walk in radical giftedness and radical love; however there is a promise that "the glory of the latter house shall be greater than that of the former" Haggai 2:9. The scripture does not teach that the generation is greater, but simply, that the glory will be greater. The thought of a generation walking in greater glory than Moses or even David may sound arrogant, but Hebrews declares:

"These were all commended for their faith, yet none of them received what had been promised, since God had planned something better for us so that only together with us would they be made perfect." Hebrews 11:39-40 NIV

The destiny of these heroes of faith will not be complete until we finish what they started, and we cannot accomplish this without His glory and presence. This is astounding! This is why this generation needs to take seriously the mandate of heaven. The mandate to preach the gospel to all creation while walking in radical love, and in wholeness in our relationships.

My prayer is that we allow the Spirit of God to shape us into containers that can carry the fullness of God. Containers that bear the fruit of His Spirit, and do the greater works Jesus prophesied would be released through us. All of this being produced out of walking in intimate fellowship with God.

[Section One]
The Nature and Character of God

Lesson 1
The New Covenant

The way we perceive God will affect the way we communicate to Him, and to people. The more time we spend with Jesus, and His word, the greater we begin to understand His nature properly. Much misrepresentation of God has come from those who do not have clear understanding of the covenant we are under, which Hebrews says is "a better covenant with greater promises" Hebrews 8:6. God has never changed, but His covenants with men have. In scriptures we see God had made a covenant with Abraham (Genesis 15:18), Noah (Genesis 9:17), David (2 Samuel 7:13), and Moses (Exodus 19-24). But the scriptures also say that when Jesus was crucified, His shed blood created a New Covenant, Luke 22:20.

The covenants God made with Abraham and David where eternal covenants we see fulfilled in Christ.

"The record of the genealogy of Jesus the Messiah, the son of David, the son of Abraham…" Matthew 1:1

Christ fulfilled the Abrahamic Covenant.

"Now the promises were spoken to Abraham and to his seed. He does not say, 'And to seeds', as referring too many, but rather to one, 'And to your seed', that is, Christ." Galatians 3:16

Christ fulfilled the Davidic Covenant.

"Your house and your kingdom shall endure before Me forever; your throne shall be established forever." 2 Samuel 7:16

"Which He promised beforehand through His prophets in the holy Scrip-

tures, concerning His Son, who was born of a descendant of David according to the flesh, who was declared the Son of God with power by the resurrection from the dead, according to the Spirit of holiness, Jesus Christ our Lord." Romans 1:2-4

"Brethren, I may confidently say to you regarding the patriarch David that he both died and was buried, and his tomb is with us to this day. And so, because he was a prophet and knew that God had sworn to him with an oath to seat one of his descendants on his throne, he looked ahead and spoke of the resurrection of the Christ, that He was neither abandoned to Hades, nor did His flesh suffer decay. This Jesus God raised up again, to which we are all witnesses. Therefore having been exalted to the right hand of God, and having received from the Father the promise of the Holy Spirit, He has poured forth this, which you both see and hear. For it was not David who ascended into heaven, but he himself says:'The Lord said to my Lord,"Sit at My right hand, until I make Your enemies a footstool for Your feet.'"" Acts 2:29-35

Jesus is seated forever on the throne of David, fulfilling God's promises to David. The Mosaic Covenant, however, was not eternal and had a shelf life:

"For Christ is the end of the law for righteousness to everyone who believes." Romans 10:4

This is important because most people are hindered in their relationship with God because they are constantly conscious of their sin, and feel unworthy to enter the presence of the Lord. The Mosaic Covenant promised that if you were able to obey, then you where blessed, but if you disobeyed you where cursed (Deuteronomy 28). The New Covenant that was made in Christ, is not based on blessings and curses, but is based in sonship. Christ is the end of the curse of the law, making us all sons and daughters (Galatians 3:13).

"For it was fitting for Him, for whom are all things, and through whom are all things, in bringing many sons to glory, to perfect the author of their salvation through suf-

ferings." Hebrews 2:10

The promise of the New Covenant is that our sins will be remembered no more, and that Christ has made a way for us beyond the veil. This is almost the complete opposite of what was promised in the Mosaic Covenant.

"For I will be merciful to their iniquities, and I will remember their sins no more." Hebrews 8:12

"Therefore, brethren, since we have confidence to enter the holy place by the blood of Jesus, by a new and living way which He inaugurated for us through the veil, that is, His flesh." Hebrews 10:19-20

In the New Covenant God has forgiven us our sins. This reveals to us that our sin may cause us to separate ourselves from God, but God does not separate Himself from us. In the book of Genesis, you will notice that after Adam and Eve sinned, they hid themselves away, but God came looking for them. In the same way, when God's people hide from shame and guilt, the Father comes looking for them.

Christ has in His flesh created a New Covenant where the law is no longer written on tablets of stone but in our minds and hearts (Hebrews 8:10). The law put a veil over the Father; Jesus came to reveal what the Father was like.

"But to this day whenever Moses is read, a veil lies over their heart; but whenever a person turns to the Lord, the veil is taken away." 2 Corinthians 3:15-16

If we want to know what the Father is like we have but to look at Jesus. Jesus declared, 'I and the Father are one', and when Phillip asked to see the Father, Jesus responded, 'Phillip how long have I been with you, and you say show us the Father?' Jesus is the expressed image of the Father (Hebrews 1:3).

A very important verse to completely understand God's heart for His people is found in Exodus:

"You yourselves have seen what I did to the Egyptians, and how I bore you on eagles' wings, and brought you to Myself. Now then, if you will indeed obey My voice and keep My covenant, then you shall be My own possession among all the peoples, for all the earth is Mine; and you shall be to Me a kingdom of priests and a holy nation.' These are the words that you shall speak to the sons of Israel."(Exodus 19:4-6)

God's original intention for His people was that they would minister directly to Him as a kingdom of priests. God was inviting all of His people to hear His voice and to serve Him directly.

"All the people perceived the thunder and the lightning flashes and the sound of the trumpet and the mountain smoking; and when the people saw it, they trembled and stood at a distance. Then they said to Moses, "Speak to us yourself and we will listen; but let not God speak to us, or we will die." Deuteronomy 20:18-19

The people feared hearing God's voice and requested a mediator. This changed the covenant offer God had made with His people. From here on you'll notice there's no longer an invitation to all of the children of Israel to hear His voice, but the Levites are raised up to represent the Lord.

Prior to this experience on Mt. Sinai, God dealt directly with His sons and daughters. After this event, a mediator and new laws were put into place. In order to live an empowered life, it's critical to have a healthy view of the nature and character of God, or we will approach God like we are at Mt. Sinai, instead of Mt. Zion.

"For you have not come to a mountain that can be touched and to a blazing fire, and to darkness and gloom and whirlwind, and to the blast of a trumpet and the sound of words which sound was such that those who heard begged that no further word be spoken to them. For they could not bear the command, "If even a beast touches the mountain, it will be stoned." And so terrible was the sight, that Moses said, "I am full of fear and trembling." But you have come to Mount Zion and to

the city of the living God, the heavenly Jerusalem, and to myriads of angels, to the general assembly and church of the firstborn who are enrolled in heaven, and to God, the Judge of all, and to the spirits of the righteous made perfect, and to Jesus, the mediator of a new covenant, and to the sprinkled blood, which speaks better than the blood of Abel." Hebrews 12:18-24

I love this same verse in the Message Bible, it says:

"Unlike your ancestors, you didn't come to Mount Sinai — all that volcanic blaze and earthshaking rumble — to hear God speak. The earsplitting words and soul-shaking message terrified them and they begged him to stop. When they heard the words — "If an animal touches the Mountain, it's as good as dead" — they were afraid to move. Even Moses was terrified. No, that's not your experience at all. You've come to Mount Zion, the city where the living God resides. The invisible Jerusalem is populated by throngs of festive angels and Christian citizens. It is the city where God is Judge, with judgments that make us just. You've come to Jesus, who presents us with a new covenant, a fresh charter from God. He is the Mediator of this covenant. The murder of Jesus, unlike Abel's — a homicide that cried out for vengeance — became a proclamation of grace." Hebrews 12:18-21 MSG

I pray for us all to have fresh eyes to see the Father through the blood of Jesus. As I have shared the revelation of God found in the New Covenant, and God's original intentions for us, I have witnessed people exhale and say, "Now I can trust the Father!"

Covenant Names of God

"For I, the Lord, do not change…" Malachi 3:6

Now we are going to explore the Covenant Names of God. I feel it is important in understanding God's nature that we know what He is called. In Hebrew culture, names were chosen very carefully as the name given would prophesy the destiny of the child. So also, God reveals His nature to us in His Covenant Names:

Yahweh

The first time God reveals His name in scripture is found in Moses' encounter at the burning bush.

"Then Moses said to God, "Behold, I am going to the sons of Israel, and I will say to them, 'The God of your fathers has sent me to you.' Now they may say to me, 'What is His name?' What shall I say to them?" God said to Moses, "I AM WHO I AM"; and He said, "Thus you shall say to the sons of Israel, 'I AM has sent me to you.'" God, furthermore, said to Moses, "Thus you shall say to the sons of Israel, 'The Lord, the God of your fathers, the God of Abraham, the God of Isaac, and the God of Jacob, has sent me to you.' This is My name forever, and this is My memorial-name to all generations." Exodus 3:13-15

God reveals Himself to Moses as 'I Am Who I Am'. Rabbinic traditions teach that God breathed as He spoke His Name. In this He was revealing Himself as a living, breathing, talking God who always was, always is and always will be. Our life and walk with God should be like breathing. The scripture teaches us that in Him we live and move and have our being. This reveals so much about the nature and character of God. He is not the God who was, He is the God who is. He is present, consistent and ever present. God will always be what the word of God says He is.

"For You have magnified Your word according to all Your name." Psalms 138:2

It's so refreshing to me to know that I can count on the nature of God to be consistent. He may change His mind but He doesn't change His nature and ways (Exodus 32:14). There are nine Compound Names of God, and each reveals the different parts of God's nature:

Jehovah Nissi – "The Lord My Banner" Exodus 17:8-16

The context of this Covenant Name came from a battle in Exodus where Amalek fought against the Children of Israel. When Moses hands where lifted up by Aaron and Hur, the children of Israel won the war, but when his hands fell down they began to loose the war. There are many applications that can be taken out of this, but the most clear is that God is our Victor. The Lord is the banner of victory over our battles. When we are facing battles in our life, remember God is our banner.

Jehovah Raah – "The Lord is My Shepherd" Psalms 23

There is much to be said about God being our shepherd. A shepherd watches over, protects, feeds and leads his sheep. When we are in need of protection, provision and guidance, we can take comfort that God is our shepherd.

Jehovah Rapha – "The Lord that Heals" Exodus 15:22-26

In every covenant, the one constant is that the Lord heals His people of sickness and disease. When the enemy tries to afflict us, we can put our hope in the healing power of God.

Jehovah Shammah – "The Lord is There" Ezekiel 48:35

The verse in Ezekiel 48:35 is a promise of the presence of the Lord abiding in the New Jerusalem. We are also told in the New Testament that we are the temples of the Holy Spirit where God's presence abides. When we feel alone, we call upon the Lord who is there.

Jehovah Tsidkenu – "The Lord Our Righteousness" Jeremiah 23:5-8

Our righteousness or right standing with God is as filthy rags. It is only the Lords righteousness imparted to us by faith in the cross of Jesus that we are in right standing with God. When the enemy tells us that we are not good enough, we get to remind Him that Jesus made us good enough to stand in the Presence of the Father.

Jehovah Mekoddishkem – "The Lord Who Sanctifies You" Leviticus 20:7-8

Holiness seems to be a bad word in the church today. Those raised in

The Nature and Character of God

a religious environment are taught to think of what they should or should not do in order to be holy before God. But in truth, when we are struggling, we are to find peace that it is the Lord who sanctifies or makes holy as we agree with Him.

Jehovah Jireh – "The Lord Will Provide" Genesis 22:1-14

The Latin word for Provide is 'pro' meaning before, and 'video' meaning to see. Literally meaning to see in advance or before the need is known. God is preparing an answer before we know that there is a need. God provided His Son for the forgiveness of our sins, but He also provides our daily bread. Whatever we have need of, all we have to do is ask.

Jehovah Shalom – "The Lord is Peace" Judges 6:24

The word 'peace' is an accurate translation, but in the Hebrew translation it means much more than peace. Shalom means completeness, wholeness, health, peace, welfare, safety, soundness, tranquility, prosperity, perfectness, fullness, rest, harmony, and the absence of agitation or discord. When we don't know what to do in a situation this name of God has the answer.

Jehovah Sabaoth – "The Lord of Hosts"

This name is mentioned several times in the scriptures. This title says several things about the nature of God and His creation, but it emphasizes God's ultimate power over the whole universe and every living creature. All of creation, and every living creature are subject to the power of God. We in turn, as His creation, exist to love and serve Him.

By meditating on each name, we learn that God is I Am. He is ever present, and never changing. He is a God who looks after lineages of those who serve Him, He is our victor, He is our Shepherd, He heals our disease, He is always with us, He is our righteousness, He sanctifies us, He will provide for us, He is the source of our peace, and He is the Lord who fights for us.

Lesson 2
The Love and Forgiveness of God

The scripture tells us that God is love. Not that God occasionally loves, but His very nature is love. Love is a very watered down word in the English language. The word love is used to describe such a vast array of emotions regarding our spouses, families, pets, movies and chocolate. In the Greek language there are four words for love. They are eros, storge, phileo and agape. Here is a brief overview of the greek definitions of the word love:

- Eros: The greek word eros is where our English word erotica is derived from. The media continually bombards our culture to make us feel like we need to be more attractive to the opposite sex. We buy cologne, get a haircut, buy more clothes, and the list goes on. The youth are hearing a message that true love is merely a physical attraction. Obviously, it is important to be attractive to the person we marry, but physical attraction is only one aspect of love. Most of our society lives in this stage of love.
- Storge: Storge is the love found in family. The love we share with our mothers, fathers, brothers, and sisters. This is a deep love, but still not the strongest love.
- Phileo: This love is best described as brotherly love. Not simply as kin but the love that causes us to reach out, help our neighbor, or help the old lady across the street.
- Agape: When the scripture says God is love, it uses this type of love. Agape is the unconditional love of God. All human love has conditions, but God's love is unconditional. He loves us just because we are. We belong to Him and it's His love and goodness that draws us to Him.

"This is how God showed his love among us: He sent his one and only Son into the world that we might live through him. This is love: not that we loved God, but that

he loved us and sent his Son as an atoning sacrifice for our sins." 1 John 4:9-10

There are two points I want to develop from these passages of scripture. 1 John 4 is almost the same as John 3:16 which states, "For God so loved the world He gave His only begotten Son, that whosoever believeth in Him will not perish but have everlasting life."

The first point I want to observe in this passage of scriptures is that God's love gives and it gives freely. Most humans, before Christ, give with the motive to get. God gave His most precious gift to mankind to bring us back to a living relationship with Him. The unselfish factor about this is that God won't force us to love Him back. The Father has given us free will. Why wouldn't He just control us, and make us serve Him? Because true love deserves a choice.

The second point I want to observe is in verse 10 of 1 John 4, stating that God first loved us, not that we loved God. He loved us and sent His Son to be the atoning sacrifice for our sins, and this demonstrates that God is the initiator of this grand love story, and would go to any length to bring us back into right relationship with Him. God's desire was to have such an intimate relationship with mankind that Jesus teaches us to call God Father. The image of an angry God dangling like a spider over the pits of hell does not rightly represent the nature of God.

1 Corinthians 13 is a passage that has reminded me often of how much I need to grow in the love of God. That was until I understood that this passage is actually describing the nature of God. When we allow the Holy Spirit to live through us in surrender, God's love is shed abroad in our hearts. We have been given the opportunity to partner with this great love.

To illustrate my point I have replaced the word love with Father God:

"Father God is patient, Father God is kind and is not jealous; Father God does not brag and is not arrogant, does not act unbecomingly; Father God does not seek its own, He is not provoked, does not take into account a wrong suffered, does not rejoice in unrighteousness, but rejoices with the truth; bears all things, believes

all things, hopes all things, endures all things. Father God never fails; but if there are gifts of prophecy, they will be done away; if there are tongues, they will cease; if there is knowledge, it will be done away. For we know in part and we prophesy in part; but when the perfect comes, the partial will be done away. When I was a child, I used to speak like a child, think like a child, reason like a child; when I became a man, I did away with childish things. For now we see in a mirror dimly, but then face to face; now I know in part, but then I will know fully just as I also have been fully known. But now faith, hope, love, abide in these three; but the greatest of these is love." 1Corinthians 13:4-13

When we understand this truth, that it is God's love for us that compels us to love others, we understand that we can't make love happen. Through growing in our knowledge and relationship with God we also grow in love. Love is one of the fruits of the Holy Spirit, and fruit grows. Love grows in us by our understanding of how much we are loved by Him.

"We love Him because He first loved us." (1 John 4:19)

As a new believer I had an experience where I saw a scene in a garden with two flaming swords blocking the way. Then the swords pulled back and I saw a hand beckon me to come and I heard a voice say," I love your presence more than you love mine." This baffled me. God loves my presence? Who is this God we serve, who loves so purely and so violently? Understanding God's love and forgiveness towards us draws us to Him. The revelation of our sinfulness pushes us away from God like it did to Adam in the garden. When we understand that Jesus took our sin on the cross and declared it is finished, this revelation should cause us to come boldly to His throne of Grace.

God's intentions with Adam remains the same for us, to walk with us in intimate friendship. It's out of this place of walking with God, spending time with God in worship, communion with the Holy Spirit, and the living Word we learn to hear His voice and learn His ways. Time spent with the Holy Spirit and His word reveal God's heart and nature. It is imperative as we embark on a journey of learning to be used to speak on behalf of God, that we learn His ways, how He speaks, how he feels, and we allow His thoughts to become ours.

The Nature and Character of God

A God of Forgiveness

I want to illustrate from scripture a story of someone who understood the power of God's forgiveness. There was a woman caught in the act of adultery. The people brought her out to stone her. Jesus spoke, "let him who has no sin cast the first stone." One by one they walked away. Then Jesus spoke to the woman and said, "Woman I don't condemn you either, now go and sin no more." Receiving forgiveness from a loving, merciful savior, releases the power that enables us to walk in victory over sin. It's the revelation of the finished work of the cross and the infilling of the Holy Spirit that empowers us to overcome.

God's Love for the One

One of the best illustrations in scripture of the goodness and forgiveness of Father God is found in the life of Peter. Peter was known to be outspoken, and a bit unpredictable. I relate the most to Peter in personality than to the other twelve. When things get too quiet, Peter was probably the first one to speak out of nervous energy. I believe Matthew 17 illustrates this when Jesus appears on the mountain with Elijah and Moses. Instead of staying quiet he blurted out, "Let's make a monument." God replied simply, "This is my Son, hear Him."

During the last supper when Jesus declares that one among them would betray Him, Peter opens his mouth again, "Not me Lord!" Jesus replies, "Peter by the time the rooster crows three times you would have denied me three times." Then Peter, consistent with his character, says "Not me God."

Peters has the amazing revelation of Jesus in Matthew 16, and then, just chapters later, is being told, "Get behind me, Satan!" because he was trying to talk Jesus out of the suffering of the cross. This was Jesus' very purpose for coming to the earth. We all know the rest of the story. Jesus is crucified and Peter fulfills the Lord's prophecy and denies Him three times.

In John 20:2-7, Peter and John hear of the emptied tomb, and they both go running to the tomb. John outruns Peter. I have to wonder what Peter was thinking on the run. How horrible he must have felt for denying the Messiah. John walks into the tomb first, and Peter hangs back. Now any doubt that Jesus was whom He said He was is removed. Peter may have thought, "He is who He says He is and I, Peter, have denied Him not once but three times."

"Very early in the morning, on the first day of the week, they came to the tomb when the sun had risen. And they said among themselves, 'Who will roll away the stone from the door of the tomb for us?' But when they looked up, they saw that the stone had been rolled away—for it was very large. And entering the tomb, they saw a young man clothed in a long white robe sitting on the right side; and they were alarmed. But he said to them, 'Do not be alarmed. You seek Jesus of Nazareth, who was crucified. He is risen! He is not here. See the place where they laid Him. But go, tell His disciples—and Peter...'" Mark 16:2-7

After Jesus was raised from the dead, an angel told those present, "Go and tell the disciples- and Peter." I love how the scripture isolates Peter, as if to say, "Peter may have forgotten me but I have not forgotten Him." All of heaven wanted Peter to know that God still loved him, and that He was thinking about him.

Jesus earlier instructed the disciples before His ascension to "Tarry and wait in Jerusalem until they receive the Promise of the Father." Peter goes fishing. Jesus calls out to them to cast their fishing net on the other side, and the net ripped, overflowing with fish.

In John 21:5-7, a very interesting conversation happens between Peter and Jesus. Jesus asks Peter if he agapao loves Him, twice. Peter replies twice that he phileo loves Him. Jesus is revealing to Peter the difference in their love for one another. The last time Jesus asks Peter if he loves Him like a dear friend or companion, Peter is grieved and replies, "Lord, you know."

There are times in each one of our lives where our hearts become aware of the shallowness of our love for God. This is always reflected in the way we live and the things we value. Peter denies Jesus three times. Jesus asks Him three times if he loves Him. For each time Peter denied Jesus, He told Him he loved Him.

Jesus' attention to single Peter out later turns Peter into one of the greatest apostles in scripture. There becomes such oneness in Peter's relationship with God that the Holy Spirit overshadows him, and everywhere he went his shadow healed the sick.

Another example of the nature of God is found in Mark. We have the story of Jesus crossing the sea with His disciples, calming the wind and the waves. What was the purpose of crossing the sea to begin with?

"And when He had come out of the boat, immediately there met Him out of the tombs a man with an unclean spirit, who had his dwelling among the tombs; and no one could bind him, not even with chains, because he had often been bound with shackles and chains And the chains had been pulled apart by him, and the shackles broken in pieces; neither could anyone tame him. And always, night and day, he was in the mountains and in the tombs, crying out and cutting himself with stones." Mark 5:2-5

Jesus then proceeds to cast out a legion of demons from the man; the man being completely delivered! Almost immediately they get back in the boat and leave. It seems the whole purpose for the trip, and even calming of the storm, was for one man to be set free! This is the nature of the God we serve. We need this revelation! When I read this story I thought, "Jesus crossed the sea for one demon possessed man; He would certainly do it for me!"

It's easy to believe in the love of God for the multitudes, but where we struggle is God's love towards us personally. These scriptures illustrate God's love for the one.

Lesson 3
God's Love for Me

My story, like Peter and the demoniac, is one of God's mercy and of God's love. I wasn't in pursuit of God, and I really did not care to know Him; however, He was in pursuit of me. As I remember back to the day the Lord saved my life, I can still feel the fear and excitement of that night. It was a Friday evening, and myself along with a few of my friends were going to Philadelphia to do some barhopping. We all chipped in to get a limo so we wouldn't be drinking and driving. We arrived, got drunk, and at 2 a.m., received a call from our limo driver. He was stuck in traffic, and he asked if we could walk to the nearest main street so he could pick us up quicker. The street that we were closest to happened to be located in a rougher section of the neighborhood. Directly across the street from where we stood waiting, there was a group of Hispanic men pushing each other around. The action began to escalate, and as the police arrived, the men took off running.

While all this action was taking place, I was standing at the end of an alleyway waiting for the limo, and being very drunk I passed out on a yellow post that was at the end of the curb. The yellow post came up to my hip, and the alley way was directly to the right of me. I passed out, but then was suddenly startled by a loud noise that sounded like a loud firecracker. At that very moment I felt something grab the back of my shirt and pull me back. I felt fire go by my forearm, and instantly I heard weeping in the distance. Looking around I saw people lying all over the sidewalk crying. I ran to check on my friends and they were all on the ground too. Then I heard, "My hip! My hip! I'm shot in my hip!" I ran over to see what had happened, and saw an African American guy holding his hip. Someone shouted my name and I realized that the limo had arrived. I ran to it as fast as I could, jumped inside, and we took off. All of this happened in a flash. I was so overwhelmed that I couldn't cry or laugh. I just put my hands over my face.

While I sat there with my hands over my face, I heard an inner audible voice which sounded like a very loud thought, "Where would you go if you died right now?" I responded, "I would die and go to hell. I'm drunk." Then the next thought came, "Where was that man shot?" I answered, "In his hip." Then I saw what would be like a video in my mind. I saw myself lying down on the yellow post. I watched as a bullet was going directly for my head, and something pulled me back so that the bullet went right over my forearm and hit another man in the hip. Something had saved my life. I had an encounter with God. Needless to say, I gave my life to the Lord a week later.

God is a God of Forgiveness. My testimony clearly reveals a God who is in pursuit of His people. I wasn't even looking for God. I thought religion was something people did when they got old, but what I found wasn't religion. I found Christ. After I asked Christ to come into my heart I felt clean. I knew I was forgiven. The gospel is so simple at times, and I think people can overlook its power. "God sent His only son into the world that knew no sin to become sin that we could be reconciled to God" (1 John 4:9). This scripture declares that our sins have been thrown into the sea of forgetfulness, and are to be remembered no more. Any God who can not only forgive, but also forgets the sins of His people, is a God worth serving with all of our being.

Testimony of the Love of God

Years ago when I was attending ministry school, I worked for a state run group home for troubled teens. I loved this job because I had the opportunity to minister to a lot of young men.

When the boys at the group home behaved themselves, they were permitted to go on outings during the weekends. So I would take them to church. On one of those weekends I brought two of the boys, Michael and Frankie, to church when Benny Perez was the guest speaker ministering. Both of these young men were involved in gang activity, and had very troubled lives. From what I had observed of them, neither of them had a relationship with the Lord. During the service I waved the youth pastor over to see if he could have Benny Perez pray for them. As it worked out, Benny Perez did come over and began to minister to them, and the power of God touched both of them. They both fell to the ground rolling and trembling under the power of the Holy Spirit. I was shocked! I was expecting that maybe they were going to receive a word of encouragement, but this was much better than I could have imagined.

When we got into the van to return them back to the group home, I started asking lots of questions. They both responded the same way. They made it clear that I wasn't allowed to tell anyone what had happened because they had cried.

A few weeks later, I received a phone call at 9 p.m. asking if I could report to work immediately. Almost a soon as I said yes and hung up the phone, I instantly got a migraine headache. Even on my way to the group home I got lost while driving, and hit a bird. What was going on? Something was definitely happening in the spirit.

As I walked in the door to the group home, there were more than normal amount of staff present, and they were all talking intently to one another. When they saw me they pulled me into the conversation, and told me to go take a look at the first room to get a grasp on all that had been happening. When I walked by the room I noticed that the door had been broken, and pieces of a dresser were stuck in the dry wall. I looked up and my eyes met the eyes of a young man who was obviously very scared and troubled mentally. I was told to leave him alone, and that they would be bringing him back to the mental hospital in the morning.

The other staff members left, and I was on duty with a staff member from Peru. We instantly hit it off sharing God stories. The disturbed young man who had destroyed the bedroom sat and listened as we shared back and forth. I felt the Lord give me a word of knowledge that this young man was being tormented in the night. So I shared it with him and offered him hope. He never engaged, but I could tell he was listening.

Some of the other boys began to overhear me telling God stories, and they all walked out with their bibles and asked if we could do a bible study. That was hard for me to turn down. Michael and Frankie were amongst the boys that had come in the room, and I asked them to share what God had done with them the night before. They looked up at me quickly, and then I realized I had forgotten that they had asked me not to tell anyone. However, Frankie said, "You can tell them". So I began to share the story, and as I did, one of the boys named Cesar said, "Man I wish today was Saturday." "Why Cesar?" I asked. "Then tomorrow would be Sunday, and I would be able to experience what they did."

I began daydreaming about laying hands on the boys, and then started thinking about the potential of nothing happening. I was beginning to be gripped with fear and unbelief. But I worked myself up into praying for Cesar, and I blurted out "Stand up!" His eyes got big, and he jumped up. I told him that I was going to lay hands on him, and that the power of God was going to come upon him, even though I was not believing anything would happen. I began to pray and invited the Holy Spirit, and BAM! The presence of God began to fall upon him, and he took a few steps back. Then he sat down, and put his hands over his eyes. I asked him, "What would you do if someone was at the door?" He quickly responded, "I would let them in." I said," Jesus is knocking on the door of your heart. Will you let him in?" And then I led him to Jesus.

The next hour was one I will never forget. I held my own revival service in a group home. We led the young men to the Lord, prayed for the infilling of the Holy Spirit, and laid hands on one another for healing. What was next to do? I ran to my car, grabbed a worship cd, and I taught the boys how to rest in the Lord.

One of the young men blurted out, "I'm in a garden!" So I ran over to him to interpret the experience, but he shouted out, "I know what it means! Jesus wants to walk with me the way He walked with Adam in the garden."

Each young man was having his own experience with God. One of the most impactful experiences was Frankie's. He started weeping and trembling under God's power. I asked if he was ok, and he asked me if I had read his file. I told him that I had not. He then began to tell me that his mother and father were both in prison for life. His mother, while high on drugs, drowned his baby sister in the bathtub because she couldn't get her to stop crying. He went on to tell me that His grandmother became his caregiver, but one morning he walked into her room to wake her, and she had passed away in her sleep.

Tears flooded his eyes as he told me that while resting in the Lord, he had a vision. He saw Jesus standing next to his grandmother, and she was holding his baby sister. It was such an emotional moment that we embraced, and wept together.

That night after sending the boys off to bed, they were noticeably different. I sat in the staff office in disbelief. Then I heard a loud exhale followed by a voice saying, "You don't know how long I've wanted to touch them, but I didn't have hands to flow through." The reality of those words from God gripped my heart. I will always remember the truth that I learned that night. It is our heavenly Father's desire to touch the broken. If He didn't need hands and feet, He could visit them himself, but He has chosen to partner with man. These young boys had encounters with Jesus that changed their lives forever.

[Section Two]
The Heart of a Prophet

Lesson 4
Friendship with God

"No longer do I call you slaves, for the slave does not know what his master is doing; but I have called you friends, for all things that I have heard from My Father I have made known to you." John 15:15

In 2004 I had a visitation from the Lord while at a meeting in Homer, Alaska. My eyes were opened, and I saw a brown mantle floating out of the sky. I was having an open vision, and I could see it with my natural eyes. The speaker at the meeting began to prophesy that he saw the Lord releasing mantles, and as he was prophesying this I could see a brown mantle shimmering and falling down. I asked the Lord what he was showing me, and then I saw an open vision of the Lord Jesus standing in front of me. The Lord spoke to me and said, "Today I call you my friend. I will make you a recognized prophet to your generation." This was one of the most life changing encounters that I have ever experienced personally. As I meditated upon the encounter, I began to ask the Lord about what this brown mantle represented, but it wasn't until some years later that He clearly brought about that answer to me.

The answer came when I had another encounter at the graduation of a bible school I had taught at. On the last day of school we decided to wash the feet of the students as a sign of humility. It was a prophetic act to say, "Blessed are the feet that bring good news. Do likewise to others." And as I was washing their feet, the spirit of the Lord came upon me, and I began to weep in the presence of the Lord. Then the Lord said to me, "Ivan, I have called you to wash the feet of the body of Christ for the rest of your life."

These two experiences have significantly impacted how I have lived as a minister of God. My life is one of friendship with God, to be a prophetic voice to a generation, and to wash the feet of the body of Christ.

In another service, the same speaker from the meeting in Homer, Alaska and I were ministering together. He gave a testimony to me that while he was teaching in the service, he could feel something like a blanket resting around his waist. The Lord began to speak to him out of John 13. The verse where Jesus says, "I come from the father, and I go to the father", and Jesus takes an apron, puts it around his waist, and he begins to wash the feet of His disciples. Out of this, he begins to hear Jesus speak to him about a mantle of friendship, and foot washing. After he finished giving this testimony, a reputable prophet came up to him and said, "I see a brown mantle resting around your waist right now", and begins to confirm all that the Lord had been speaking to him.

As I heard this testimony, the power of God began to come upon me because it was the same color mantle, and the exact same passage of scripture that the Lord had spoken to me previously. It all related to the washing of feet. I began to see that the Lord was not just commissioning me, but commissioning a generation. What the Lord wants to do is raise up a people that will have an understanding that the prophetic ministry is a ministry that is to wash the feet of the body of Christ. It is a ministry that is called to walk in a place of humility and servanthood, and to function out of a place of friendship with God.

"Pursue Love, and earnestly desire spiritual gifts. Especially that you might prophecy."1 Corinthians 14:1

When I was younger I remember asking one of my pastors why, above all gifts, Paul says we are to pursue prophecy. Why not healing? When we look at the scriptures, Jesus moved mostly in healing, and miracles. He asked me, "Think about it Ivan. How do you receive a true prophetic word?" and I said, "Well, you hear the voice of God." And he said, "Exactly! So above all things, and above all gifts, desire to hear His voice, and to speak His heart. "

Humility in the heart of a prophetic minister has to be number one. We also have to have a real relationship with the Word so that we can rightly communicate the nature and character of God. Secondly, we have to have a sensitive heart to Jesus, and a genuine love for people. When the spirit of God speaks to us, He shouldn't have to yell at us. He should only have to speak quietly, and we hear. There is a passage in Isaiah that says, "God dwells with those that are humble of heart, and that tremble at his word." When a prophetic individual grows in the gifts of the spirit without growing in humility, this is where it becomes dangerous. The individual may start to feel like maybe they are receiving prophetic revelation because they are more anointed then everybody else, or maybe they are better than other people. They forget that the Lord can speak through the mouth of a donkey if He needs to, and the bible says even the rocks will praise him. We need to understand that as a mouthpiece for the Lord, we not only want to speak what the Father is saying, but we want to rightly reflect his heart.

In the encounter I had where the Lord was speaking to me about washing the feet of His people, and Him calling to me to be His friend, I began to realize something. In John 15:15 it says, "I no longer call you servants, but I call you friends. For a servant doesn't know what his master is doing, but to a friend I reveal my secrets." In the Old testament God used a lot of people. When I say used, I mean that he anointed, or His spirit rested upon them, but he called very few His friends. Abraham was a prophet, and he was called a friend of God. The bible says that Abraham looked for a city in which its builder and maker was God. So when God spoke to Abraham, he obeyed God's word. God said to Abraham, "Look at the stars and see how many your descendants will be. Look at the sands of the seashore, so will your descendants will be." Abraham began to hope beyond hope it says in Romans, and out of that faith Abraham became a friend of God. Out of Abraham's radical faith, and obedience to God, he became known as friend.

In the Book of Job, there is a passage that says, "The friendship of God was over his tent" (Job 29:4). This is so amazing! This meant that the intimate, secret friendship of God was over his tent.

Another great example is in Numbers 33 regarding Moses, it says,

"Some prophets I speak to in mystery, dark riddles and sayings, but not so to my servant Moses. I talk to him face to face, as a friend speaks to a friend." In Exodus 33:11 it refers to Moses as a friend of God.

Abraham, Job and Moses, are great examples of those that not only understood the deeds of God, but also understood the ways of God. When God was going to judge Sodom and Gomorrah, Abraham petitioned God. He asked God if there were ten righteous, would He relent. Abraham moved the heart of God because of their relationship, and Abraham's response to God.

The same thing happened in the story of Moses. Moses began to interact with God in a unique way. Moses still had a fear of God, he still honored God, but he felt free to question the voice of God regarding the children of Israel without fearing that God might smite him. Moses' interaction actually moved the heart of God. Psalms 103 says, "The children of Israel knew Gods deeds, but Moses knew his ways." This is what it means to be a friend of God. It means that we know His secrets, and understand His mysteries.

"Call unto me and I will answer you, and I will show you great and mighty things." *Jeremiah 33:3*

In Hebrews this scripture says, "Call unto me and I will answer you, and I will show you mysteries." Some people have those rare sovereign encounters with the Lord, and those are amazing, but then there are those that get a steady stream of revelation from God. We may begin to wonder, "What is it about those individuals that they continue to get so much revelation, while others get only the rare encounter?" I believe it comes down to the fact that a friend of God will ask God questions. In a developing friendship, you ask questions to get more acquainted with the other person. You don't just sit there and experience a friend, you interact with them. This is critical for a friendship to grow.

In Psalms 91 it says that there is "the secret place of the most High".

When we look back at the story of Moses, God established the tent of meeting outside the camp. I always found it interesting that people had to go out of their home to go meet with God, but now under the New Covenant we have the ability to have that secret place with God. Secret places have secret entrances, and the bible talks about prayer being one of those entrances. We all need to have a secret place where we meet with the Lord.

We are learning to develop a relationship with God through prayer, and we are learning to ask questions, but then we must also learn to listen. Psalms 46:10 says, "Be still and know that I am God". We need to learn to allow the Lord to speak back. A critical part of being in relationship with the Lord is allowing him to speak back to us, and encourage, direct and correct us. This is the place with the Lord where we learn how to worship and praise. As we 'hang out' with Jesus, we begin to glorify him, and magnify him, and begin to see him as he is.

Lesson 5
Character, Credibility & Favor

Character

When Jesus was walking on the shores of the Sea of Galilee He saw two fishermen, Peter and Andrew, and invited them to follow him. Matthew 4:19 says, "Follow me, and I will make you fishers of men." Peter and Andrew left everything, and laid down their livelihood to follow Jesus. These men weren't hobby fisherman. They were the sons of Zebedee, and fishing was the family business. It is true that Jesus was a miracle worker and that he moved in power, but there had to be more that these two men saw in Jesus than just power for them to have surrendered it all as they did. It was the Character and person of Jesus that drew men to Him.

It is essential that we grow in Character, but we also have to have the patience and the understanding that it takes time to develop that Character. I gave my life to Jesus at twenty years old, and before that I had a lifestyle with much brokenness. I had to grow in my relationship with the Lord, and grow in an understanding of sonship and identity. There are some Christians that were raised in Christian homes, and grew up with Godly morals and values. They maybe went to church, and had experiences with God at a young age. These different life experiences mean that a different level of Character has to be developed. Character is not something you can get through impartation or the laying on of hands. Character is something that is developed over time, through the trials of our lives, and growing in our personal understanding of what our triggers and hooks may be. Character grows when we begin to recognize those areas that the enemy has tried to establish strongholds, and we allow the Holy Spirit to do a work in our hearts and lives. In order for the Holy Spirit to do a work in our lives, we need time building a relationship with God so that the fruit of the Spirit begins to grow. "Abide in Me, and I in you. As the branch cannot bear fruit of itself unless it abides in the vine, so neither can you unless you abide in me." (John 15:4). The fruit of the spirit comes from abiding in intimacy with Jesus.

It requires time in order to really know someone's character. We have all encountered individuals with bad character, but they can still move in power. It is usually only a matter of time before people begin to see the lack of Godly fruit coming from their lives. As ministers that are called to have influence over people, it is important that we have allowed the time it takes for God to develop our Character. Anyone can smile, and put on a show. The bible says that Satan was an Angel of Light, but was a deceiver and a liar. When we are moving in the gifts of the Holy Spirit, in the prophetic anointing, often people can be more skeptical. There has to be more accountability and Character developed in a person who moves in influence and power, than someone who doesn't, and this takes time. It isn't enough to have a position of authority or a title to begin speaking into people's lives. People need to know that we care about them, and that we are going to walk with them. We will not have influence when we prophesy, or the right kind of influence, if we are lacking in Character. Character equals time.

Credibility

It can take a long time before people will start to trust a minister or ministry to hear the voice of God for life choices or ministry decisions. That is not something that we trust just anyone to do. Credibility, just like Character also equals time, and a lifestyle of faithfulness. There has to be the evidence that we are walking in a fruitful and established relationship with Jesus, and this is evident when a person is in relationship with God.

What kind of relationship do we have with the Body of Christ? It is essential and important that we have healthy relationships with man in order for Credibility to be established. Many times I have had traveling ministers ask if they could come and minister in my church. They always have an amazing resume to share with me, and exploit to tell me about. All these things are probably true, but outside of a relationship with them, unless the Lord tells me otherwise, I won't have them come and speak. The reason is because as a shepherd it is my responsibility to protect the sheep. Especially with prophetic ministers, I need to know who they are, and if they have Character. Are they having problems in their life, are they having marital issues, and if so, are they working on them? Are they allowing people to speak into their lives? Are they a part of a local church? Do they have community? These are important things to know if they are going to establish Credibility as ministers.

Favor

"Favor Ain't Fair" – TD Jakes

The bible says of both Samuel and Jesus that they grew in Favor and stature with both God and man. We can grow in Favor. It is true that God loves all of us equally, but we are not all favored the same. All you have to do is look at the scriptures to see that this is true. John was the only one that rested his head on the chest of Jesus. Often times we look and wonder why another person seems to have a greater measure of favor. David was a man after Gods own heart, though he made a lot of mistakes. In Acts 13:22 it says that David accomplished the purposes of God for his generation. So David, in the midst of all his weakness, was still a man after Gods own heart.

God is the one that gives Favor, and this is very challenging for people to understand. It's especially hard for the North American church, because we are accustomed to the 'American Dream' and pushing our way to the top. We push and work our way through our education and degrees to become more successful, and then we develop an entitlement mindset that can cause the belief that we deserve all we worked for; however, this is not the case with God. God grows our Favor with both God and Man, and this is important to understand.

Some of us may have a great amount of Favor to prophesy within the setting of a home group, but maybe when we try to prophetically minister on a Sunday morning we are not allowed that platform by leadership. In this scenario, the problem can become that our pride wells up and we begin to criticize the pastor and the leadership, accusing them of being controlling. Then, that offense can cause us to leave and go to another congregation, and the cycle continues. Then we can enter the category that I like to call "The Doner's". The Doner's are those that are DONE with the institution of church. The truth is that they have not allowed the process of the Holy Spirit to work in their lives, and so they blame others. If they had learned the process of Character, Credibility and Favor, it would have saved them the offense, and allowed them to mature more into their gifting.

The Lord may give someone Favor in the local church, and they become known as a prophet to that local body of believers. They have been given the authority and Favor to speak the prophetic words the Lord is giving them, and have Credibility with the people locally. However, the same individual may not have the same amount of Favor to speak out prophetically over regions or the nation. God is the only one that creates this kind of platform and Favor.

It is critical that we begin to understand that we may be functioning with a Gift of Prophecy, and may have a desire to prophesy over rulers and kings, but without the Favor the Lord brings, we will have no platform to release it. If God has placed a desire within our hearts to prophesy over people of influence and governments, then God will cause it to come to fulfillment. But we cannot be impatient, jealous and frustrated because no one is listening to us. We have to remember that it takes time for the Lord to develop the Character, Credibility and Favor that is required to have that kind of influence. We have to be able to steward the voice of God in our lives, and be willing to cooperate with the refining process that we need to go through to get there.

Lesson 6
Hooks and Mixture

Hooks

"Satan comes for me, but he has nothing in me" John 14:30 NASB

We need to be a people that have nothing that the enemy can hook. When you go fishing you take bait, and in John Bevere's book, 'The Bait of Satan', he teaches that the enemy likes to use the 'bait' of offense. The enemy's goal is to create an offense that causes a root of bitterness to grow, because he knows that a root of bitterness defiles many. The enemy throws hooks into areas of our heart that are not yielded to the Lord, and as long as we do not yield these areas, the enemy will have the ability to reel us in.

A great example of this is in the life of a man by the name of John Alexander Dowie. Dowie was known for his amazing healing ministry during the early 1800's. At the height of his ministry, he was known as a man who walked in a great level of humility, and was known as a humble servant of the Lord. It is recorded that John G. Lake received an impartation of healing through Dowie's ministry, as well as healing for his family. Some history books say that there were two self-proclaimed prophets that brought a prophetic word to Dowie. They said that John Alexander Dowie was the next Elijah prophesied to return. Dowie originally responded by standing up and rebuking them publically, but there was something in his heart that clung onto the word. Dowie started out his ministry living very humbly, but by the end of his life he was dressing as a high priest, and was proclaiming that he was indeed the Elijah prophesied to come.

We need to take into consideration the lives of the men that preceded us like John Alexander Dowie, and how they started off walking in great humility unto the Lord; however, in the end they allowed Satan to wreak havoc in their lives. If we are not yielded to the Lord, and are not walking in a continual lifestyle of repentance, then the enemy will take the opportunities we give him to sow seeds that can bear bad fruit and trap people. Repentance is not just turning away from sin, but the changing of the mind.

If we want to avoid having Hooks in our heart, we need to learn to have the wisdom God gives us to reveal what is in our heart. It's critical for our emotional health. The bible guarantees that offense will come, but you do not have to choose to take offense. The Lord can use the trigger of offense to reveal something in our heart that needs to be dealt with, and bring wholeness. The enemy will use offense to cause us to become bitter. So when we become triggered and feel angry, sad, lonely or depressed, and we choose to allow ourselves to become offended, then we have positioned ourselves to become a victim that blames others for the negative feelings we have. It is our responsibility to steward the garden of our heart. When we begin to feel those negative feelings, we are being given the opportunity to pause for a moment, and reflect with the Holy Spirit about what is happening in our heart and emotions.

There is an acronym that is used in Alcoholics Anonymous called H.A.L.T: Hungry, Angry, Lonely, and Tired. When you feel these emotions, you are supposed to halt. This Acronym is very helpful for people when they are being triggered by these emotions to learn to stop and recognize what is going on inside of their heart. The bible says in Psalms 4:4, "Be angry and sin not". Did you know that anger is not a sin? The trick is to be angry but not sin. If we harbor anger and hang onto angry thoughts towards an individual, thoughts like how we may want to hurt them or want revenge, then it becomes a sin.

Mixture

When I was about 20 years old, and I had just given my life to the Lord, I went to a really inspiring men's retreat. The retreat launched me into an incredible spiritual high, and caused a real hunger for the Lord to burn in me. After returning from the retreat I went to a Sunday morning service. During the part of the service when they started taking the offering, people began to walk up to put money in the offering baskets, and an older woman walked past me. Instantly, I saw her completely naked in my imagination. This was so odd because she wasn't even a young or attractive woman to me. I physically reacted to what I had seen in my mind's eye, and put my hands over my face. It was completely demonic, and I began to be overwhelmed with emotions of shame. I thought to myself, "I'm not a man of God, and this whole week at the retreat was for nothing. How can I be a man of God and have these kinds of thoughts?" I felt guilt and shame attacking me, and as this was happening, an elder of the church approached me. He said that he felt like the Lord told him to come over and check on me. I didn't want to tell him what had been going on, but finally he got me to tell him. He smirked at me and he said, "Ivan, don't you know what that is?" I said, "No!" He said to me, "I can only imagine that you had a past before you gave your life to Christ, and now the enemy is trying to pull up some of the things you struggled with in your past so that you would feel shame and guilt. That's the enemy!" He began to tell me his testimony, prayed for me, and broke off the lies of the enemy. Because I had those images in my head from before I was saved, the enemy was able to pull those things up, and try to use them against me.

"But present yourselves to God as those alive from the dead, and your members as instruments of righteousness to God." Romans 6:13

We need to have an understanding of what it looks like to have Mixture in our heart if we are going to operate in the prophetic anointing. We must learn how to yield our members to the Lord; Our members being our eyes, ears, heart, mind, mouth and our hands unto righteousness. Job 33:33 says, "I made a covenant with my eyes not to lust after a woman." If we have a gifting as a seer, and the Lord uses us prophetically to minister to people, then we hear the voice of the Lord with our eyes. So then if we are not careful to yield our eyes unto righteousness, and are not careful what we see, then the enemy can actually begin to use these things in our imagination. What begins to happen is a hindrance develops in our authority when we are moving in the anointing of the Holy Spirit. The enemy will constantly try to cause us to sin in the areas we have not yielded to righteousness, or he will try to bring up our past to make us feel guilt or shame. The bible says that "out of the abundance of the heart, the mouth speaks". It is our responsibility as prophetic individuals to guard our heart. There is a level of consecration that we have to live in, and walk in as yielded vessels if we want to minister to the people of God.

So how do we yield our members to avoid Mixture in our heart? First, we are to walk in Purity. We do this by yielding our members unto righteousness as the scripture commands us. As we dedicate our entire lives to the Lord we invite His counsel into every aspect of our lives. This might mean that if the shows we love to watch aren't shows we would watch if Jesus were in the room, we might need to consider changing what's on the tube. This is what it means for His kingdom and will to be done in our lives. We need to have Purity with our eyes, ears, and with our heart, not only to be a good Christian but also to be those who have integrity in the calling and anointing Christ has called us to. Constant compromise leads to our standards lowering, and can open the door for a spirit of deception to enter in.

The second area where we can allow Mixture is in our opinions. We have so many opinions about politics and theology. If we are not careful, we may form opinions that are so strong, that when the Lord begins to speak to us contrary to what then we have believed, then our own opinion will begin to wrestle with the truth that God is trying to speak. This area of Mixture requires a sense of humility and surrender to overcome.

Let me give you an example of a word the Lord gave me for a woman in a meeting that once challenged my own personal opinion. In the meeting I walked by a woman who looked like a normal middle-aged woman. The Lord spoke to me and said; "Tell her it's ok for her to collect food stamps in this season." I honestly didn't think it was my business to say anything, and I do agree that we all go through seasons where we need assistance, but the prideful part of me was having a very hard time okaying her receiving assistance. I decided to be obedient; I stopped the woman, and told her the word the Lord had given me. Her jaw dropped and tears hit her eyes. She then began to tell me that she was a single mother, and that her job didn't provide enough income for her to live on. She was considering assistance, but her father discouraged it. If I would have allowed my own opinions to get in the way, I would have never delivered a word that brought so much freedom to this struggling single mother.

We also have to be careful that we do not have Mixture in our heart because of the people we are ministering to. It is our job as prophetic ministers to cover those we minister to by having integrity in our heart. When we are ministering prophetically over someone, his or her heart can become very open and vulnerable. Especially if our prophetic words are accurate, then their heart can begin to open to our heart. Their spirit becomes open to receiving from the Lord, a hunger for the truth grows, and a hunger for hearing what the Father would say to them grows. Our gifting and callings are without repentance, and if we are living a life of compromise, then that individual may be affected by that Mixture. Part of the prophetic word will be from the Lord, and the other part might be coming from a place of hurt or offense within us.

Let's just say that a prophetic minister has been deeply hurt by the established church, and the Lord begins to give him a prophetic word that an individual is called to be a pastor of a church. Now the potential dilemma could be that the Lord shows them specifics in the prophetic word about the individual tending the Lord's flock and feeding His sheep, but the prophetic minister has a bitter root of judgment in regards to this kind of ministry. So, then they may begin to struggle delivering the word with the purity that honors and blesses the way the Lord intended, and then worst of all things, end up hurting the individual with the word the Lord intended to release blessing. If the Lord had intended to release healing into the individual, the Mixture in the prophetic minister's heart may have completely hindered this. It is so vital that we are prepared in our hearts so that when "Satan comes to me, he has nothing in me" John 14:30.

[Section Three]
Spirit Talk: The Language of the Holy Spirit

Lesson 7
Filter of Cessationism

One of the hindrances the church faces today in being able to clearly hear the voice of God, and experience His presence, is a teaching called Cessationism.

The filter of Cessationism is a teaching that originates out of a passage in 1 Corinthians which says,

"Love never fails; but if there are gifts of prophecy, they will be done away; if there are tongues, they will cease; if there is knowledge, it will be done away. For we know in part and we prophesy in part; but when perfect comes, the partial will be done away." 1 Corinthians 13:8-10

The group that teaches on the belief of Cessationism can be referred to as Cessationists. This understanding is that the gifts will have ceased 'when perfect comes'. Cessationist's interpretation of the word 'perfect' in this verse means the canonization of the bible.

As we begin to study the history of the canonization of scripture, we understand that there were certain standards on how the books of the bible were chosen. The first standard was whether or not the books were worth dying for? During the time of the reign of the Roman Emperor Diocletian (AD 284-305), Christian's where told to burn all of their books, and sacrifice to the gods or die. The books the early churches were willing to hide and protect, at the cost of their own lives, ultimately became the 66 books of the bible. The second standard was of authorship. All of the books of the New Testament were to be written by first century apostles. So when you look at the 66 books of the bible, there is continuity and a flow. Books like The Book of Thomas, and other gnostic gospels, were not canonized because they didn't measure up to those standards.

Is there any place in scripture that foretells that there would be 66 books of the bible? If there were, wouldn't it increase our faith in the credibility of the scriptures? Well it is in scripture! In Exodus 25, Moses receives instructions from God to build the tabernacle, and what was to go inside of it. In those instructions included the building of the candlestick, mentioned in verse 31:

"Make a lampstand of pure gold. Hammer out its base and shaft, and make its flowerlike cups, buds and blossoms of one piece with them. Six branches are to extend from the sides of the lampstand-three on one side and three on the other. Three cups shaped like almond flowers with buds and blossoms are to be on one branch, three on the next branch, and the same for all six branches extending from the lampstand. And on the lampstand there are to be four cups shaped like almond flowers with buds and blossoms. One bud shall be under the first pair of branches extending from the lampstand, a second bud under the second pair, and a third bud under the third pair- six branches in all. The buds and branches shall all be of one piece with the lampstand, hammered out of pure gold." Exodus 25:31-36 NIV

The branches of the candlestick have cups, buds and blossoms. Every branch on the left side of the candlestick has three cups, three buds, and three blossoms. This pattern repeats on each of the branches. Now we know there were a total of nine cups, nine buds, and nine blossoms on either side of the candlestick. Also included on the candlestick, going directly down the middle, are four cups, four buds, and four blossoms. So, on the left side we find (9+9+9+12) totals 39, while the right side (9+9+9) equals 27. It's no mistake that there are 39 books in the Old Testament, and 27 books in the New Testament. In Psalms 119:105 it says, "Your word is a lamp to my feet and a light to my path." The candlestick is a type and shadow of the word of God that illuminates our path. There is no question in my mind that the bible was inspired by God, and then penned through the hands of men completely dependent upon the Spirit.

There are two primary views within the teaching of Cessationism. The first view being, because of the canonization of the scriptures, we have the bible. Now because of that fact, we no longer need the gifts of the spirit because the 'perfect', representing the word of God, has come. The understanding was that the Holy Spirit was moving, and moving in power, up until the canonization of scripture in AD 397, then ceased. If you study church history, you will see that miracles did not cease. During the dark ages, many of the desert fathers were moving in the miraculous. Saint Patrick, along with so many others, walked in not only the gifts of the Spirit, but had encounters with the living Christ. There are many testimonies of miracles after the bible was canonized. The only explanation Cessationists could give for all the evidence of God's power after the bible was canonized, was that the source of power was either not God, or in some circumstances, it was only a sovereign act of God that shouldn't be expected to happen often.

The second view of Cessationism, is the belief that the gifts of the Spirit ceased after the death of the last apostle. The problem with this theology is that biblically there were 22 apostles. This theology is only taking into consideration the original 12. On top of which, there is also no historical evidence of when John the Revelator died. The Bible says in Hebrews 13:8 that, "Jesus is the same yesterday, today and forever". In the Old Testament the name for God is Yaweh, which means, "I am, that I am and always will be the self existing one". Then there is the compound name of God, Jehovah Jireh, "I am the one that healeth thee". So this means that if we just look at the Old Testament perspective, that he is a God that heals yesterday, today and forever, then it is biblical to see that gifts and miracles are for today.

The filter of Cessationism would say that God can heal if it is His will, but if we look at the life of Jesus and how he taught, preached and ministered, Jesus ministered in power and healing. Acts 1:8 says, "You shall receive power when the Holy Spirit comes upon you". One definition of power is moral excellence. This is the power of God that helps us to overcome sin, and it is also God's miraculous power for healing. Romans 1:16 says, "I am not ashamed of the gospel, it is the power of God and salvation". The word 'salvation' in this text is soterio, which is the means to be saved, and the means to be delivered. Also in the book of Acts 2:21 it says, "Call upon the name of the Lord then you shall be saved". The word 'saved' in this passage means Sozo, which means healed and delivered. This clearly reveals how weak the filter of Cessationism really is when compared to the full Word of God. However, many Christians believe this way.

"The same spirit that raised Jesus from the Dead, lives with us and brings life to our mortal bodies." Romans 8:11

The same Spirit that flowed through Jesus now abides on the inside of us doing the same works that Jesus did while on the earth. 1 Corinthians 12 teaches us about the gifts of the Holy Spirit, and to not be ignorant of them. It then goes directly into 1 Corinthians 13 which is called The Love Chapter. It is in that chapter that Paul begins to teach that when the 'perfect' comes, we will no longer need prophecy, tongues and even knowledge. This is where we discover a problem in 1 Corinthians 14:1 where Paul says, "Pursue love and earnestly desire the spiritual gifts, especially that you may prophesy."

Directly after teaching that there will come a time when gifts will cease, he goes on to teach on how important it is to desire spiritual gifts, especially prophecy.

So what does it mean when Paul says, "When 'perfect' comes"? Well, that's actually simple. It is the second coming of Christ. When Christ comes we will no longer need prophecy. We will no longer need to be healed because there will be no sickness or disease in heaven. We will no longer need words of wisdom, and we will no longer need words of knowledge because Christ has come. So that's the perfect!

For now we abide in faith, hope and love. These are the three eternal virtues. So there will still be faith, hope and love in eternity, which is a pretty interesting thought. But as for today, the Gifts of the Holy Spirit are still in operation, and the power of the Holy Spirit must be demonstrated to see people come to Christ.

"When I came to you, I didn't come with eloquence of speech or human wisdom but I came with a demonstration of the Spirit's power so that faith would not rest on the wisdom of men, but on the power of God." 1 Corinthians 2:4-5

This is what we want! We want to see the power God manifested out of love, and compassion, so that people of faith will not rest on the wisdom of men. The wisdom of men being humanism and rationalism, which I believe are the god's of this age. We want the wisdom of God, so that we would once again believe in the supernatural power of God.

Lesson 8
Manifestation of the Gifts of the Spirit

"Now about the gifts of the Spirit, brothers and sisters, I do not want you to be uninformed." 1 Corinthians 1:12

This scripture points out that it is almost as if the Apostle Paul knew that the Gifts of the Spirit would be an area that would be greatly misunderstood, not only during his day, but in ours as well. Denominations have been formed and split surrounding the subject of the gifts of the Spirit, specifically the gift of tongues. Regardless of what side of the fence we choose to take on the gifts, they are still in operations today, and should be apart of the lives of everyday believers.

The Gifts of the Spirit are critical for living an empowered life. In my experience, when discussing spiritual gifts in action, most believers tend to think of a church holding a revival service; however, most of my favorite stories about the gifts in operation happened in the lives of everyday believers. For example, a mother might receive a word of knowledge to help her children get break through, or a business man may receive a word of wisdom that brings direction on where he should take his business. I have even personally experienced how the gifts of the Spirit have impacted my own workplace, and brought revelation to the management. It is important to understand that the gifts of the Spirit are always in operation, not just when we are at church, but in our everyday lives.

"Now to each one the manifestation of the Spirit is given for the common good." 1 Corinthians 12:7

The Gifts of the Spirit aren't to make us famous. The gifts of the Spirit are to serve one another. I love how this verse is written in the NLT translation:

"A spiritual gift is given to each of us so we can help each other."1 Corinthians 12:7 NLT

We are to have our hearts aligned with God's word, so that we properly understand what the motivation of our heart should be when operating in the Gifts of the Spirit towards others. In times when God's gifts are used in humility and love, they bring healing, hope and encouragement to those receiving. However, when the gifts of the Spirit are used for selfish gain or selfish motivations, the effects can be devastating. The person receiving may have been blessed in the moment, but after a while the motives of the minister may be revealed, and in turn used to discredit the move of the Spirit.

"To one person the Spirit gives the ability to give wise advice; to another the same Spirit gives a message of special knowledge. The same Spirit gives great faith to another, and to someone else the one Spirit gives the gift of healing. He gives one person the power to perform miracles, and another the ability to prophesy. He gives someone else the ability to discern whether a message is from the Spirit of God or from another spirit. Still another person is given the ability to speak in unknown languages, while another is given the ability to interpret what is being said. It is the one and only Spirit who distributes all these gifts. He alone decides which gift each person should have." 1 Corinthians 12:8-11 NLT

In this verse above, we see listed the Gifts of the Prophet. These gifts are the word of wisdom, word of knowledge and the discerning of spirits. Are you surprised that the gift of prophecy isn't found on that list? Prophecy is obviously one of the gifts that a prophetic individual would operate under, but it will become clearer by the end of this chapter what is considered to be the true gift of prophecy, according to the apostle Paul. But now, we are going to break down the three gifts from 1 Corinthians 12.

"The Gifts of the Spirit are like the rainbow, we can see the different colors but we cannot separate them from one another." Derek Prince

Word of Knowledge

A Word of Knowledge is not human knowledge, or book smarts. A word of knowledge is a supernatural knowledge from the Lord regarding someone's past or present. One of the clearest words of knowledge in Jesus ministry is found in John 4.

"He told her, "Go, call your husband and come back." "I have no husband," she replied. Jesus said to her, "You are right when you say you have no husband. The fact is, you have had five husbands, and the man you now have is not your husband. What you have just said is quite true." "Sir," the woman said, "I can see that you are a prophet." John 4:16-18

By this one word of knowledge we later see:

"Then, leaving her water jar, the woman went back to the town and said to the people, "Come, see a man who told me everything I ever did. Could this be the Messiah?" They came out of the town and made their way toward him." John 4:28-30

And then in verse 39 it says:

Many of the Samaritans from that town believed in him because of the woman's testimony, "He told me everything I ever did." John 4:39

The Word of Knowledge can be a powerful gift when used in to bring people to Christ. I have experienced the power of the word of knowledge gift both in the church as well as on the streets. I attended a youth conference, and I received a word of knowledge about a woman who had injured her back in the L4. Then I commanded healing to come into her body in Jesus name. As I was walking away from her, I heard the Lord speak again and tell me that she had a problem in her hips as well, and that I was to command healing again. Her head remained down as she was being ministered to by the Holy Spirit. She didn't confirm the word of knowledge, but I was also operating out of the gift of faith (which we will talk about more in this lesson), so it was not necessary in that moment to receive the affirmation. Later the woman testified of the accuracy of the words of knowledge, and that both of her injuries had occurred during the births of her children. In one moment the Lord had healed them both.

The word of knowledge flows in my ministry quite often partnered with the gift of healing, or the gift of prophecy. The example above demonstrates how the word of knowledge can increase faith to receive healing. We will look in more in depth at the power of the word of knowledge partnered with the gift of prophecy later, but simply put, the word of knowledge can increase the atmosphere of faith by causing people to be made aware that God knows everything about them.

Word of Wisdom

The Word of Wisdom reveals the mind of God for a future situation. Knowledge reveals, and wisdom directs. The bible is filled with words of wisdom, and one example is of Jesus' word of wisdom to Peter in Matthew 26:34 where Jesus declared that Peter would deny Him three times. Agabus also received a word of wisdom in Acts:

"After we had been there a number of days, a prophet named Agabus came down from Judea. Coming over to us, he took Paul's belt, tied his own hands and feet with it and said, "The Holy Spirit says, 'In this way the Jewish leaders in Jerusalem will bind the owner of this belt and will hand him over to the Gentiles.'" Acts 21:10-11

The word of wisdom is the ability to see what will happen in the future. The wisdom helps people to see what will happen, and often how to prepare for what is to come.

Gift of Prophecy

The Word of Wisdom and the Gift of Prophecy are often confused. Most people call everything revelatory "prophetic". Prophecy carries elements of the future, and in this, the Lord will often allow the prophetic minister to see His heart as well as His plans for an individuals life. So the prophetic gift coupled with the word of wisdom helps to give direction to the prophetic word.

This would be a good time to define the gift of prophecy. The word prophecy is prophetiea, which means to speak for the mind and counsel of God. Prophecy is both fore-telling and forth-telling. The word forth-telling means to tell forth or proclaiming. A good example of forth-telling would be the preaching of a rhema word from God, which is called prophetic preaching. Fore-telling, on the other hand, is predictive in nature, and can happen in preaching or through a public prophetic word.

John Wimber, founder of the Vineyard Association of Churches, defined prophecy this way, "Prophecy is declaring the message of God to His Church for the purpose of edification. It is not a skill, aptitude or talent. It is the actual speaking forth of words given by the Spirit in a particular situation and ceases when the words (given by the Spirit) cease. This may be given in a poetic form or even in a song."

Kenneth Hagin, founder of Rhema Bible School says, "Prophecy is supernatural utterance in a known tongue. The Hebrew word "to prophesy" means "to flow forth". It also carries with it the thought "to bubble forth like a fountain, to let drop, to lift up, to tumble forth, and to spring forth." The Greek word that is translated "prophesy" means "to speak for another". It means to speak for God or to be His spokesman."

Derek Prince, a prolific bible teacher and author says that, "The gift of prophecy is the supernaturally imparted ability to hear the voice of the Holy Spirit and speak God's mind or counsel. Prophecy not only ministers to the assembled group of believers, but also to individuals."

Its three main purpose are to:

1. Edify - build up, strengthen; make more effective,

2. Exhort - stimulate, encourage, admonish, and
3. Comfort - cheer up.

The Three Levels of Prophetic Ministry

First Level of Prophecy –The Spirit of Prophecy:

There are three levels of prophetic ministry. The first level is operating under the Spirit of Prophecy. The Spirit of Prophecy gives us all the ability to prophesy one to another so that we might learn. 1 Samuel 10:10 tells us that the Spirit of the Lord came upon Saul, and he began prophesying among the prophets. Saul comes near the prophets, and he begins to prophesy, but Saul was not a prophet. Often times this is what happens when we gather as a group of believer's in the presence of the Lord. During worship or ministry, the spirit of prophecy is poured out, and people begin to prophecy, see visions, and hear the voice of God.

This level of prophecy is available to all of us. We are all able to prophesy when the Holy Spirit pours out the prophetic anointing upon us; however, this is a specific type of prophecy. This prophecy is what Paul is talking about in 1 Corinthians 14:3 where it says, "The purpose of the prophetic ministry is for edification, exhortation and comfort."

Second Level of Prophecy – The Gift of Prophecy:

I Corinthians 12 talks about the different giftings that the Lord has distributed to the body of believers, and the Gift of Prophecy is one of them. This gifting requires a greater level of maturity, and this is the maturity that develops the Character, Credibility and Favor that I talked about previously. This gift flows more quickly than others, and does not have to wait for the Spirit of Prophecy. The Gift of Prophecy will receive prophecy for people and for churches within their sphere of influence or community.

Third Level of Prophecy – The Function of a Prophet:

The difference between the 1 Corinthians 12 Gift of Prophecy, and the Ephesians 4:11 Prophet ("God gives some to be apostles, prophets, evangelists, pastors, and teachers") is platform and influence. For example, the Lord can speak to somebody with a Gift of Prophecy regarding the president, but the president may never get that word because of a lack of favor, platform or influence. The Prophet will receive that word, and the Lord will begin to open the doors to take that prophecy to presidents, kings, ambassadors, and rulers.

After understanding the true definition of prophetic ministry, it should make sense why the scripture says:

"For you can all prophesy in turn so that everyone may be instructed and encouraged." 1 Corinthians 14:31

Prophetic Guidelines

The Gifts of the Spirit call out healing, hope and deliverance when used properly. Sadly, they aren't always used the way the Father intends them to be used. This may be confusing, but Romans 11:29 states that the gifts and callings are without repentance. Meaning, someone can fall away from Jesus, and still move very accurately and powerfully in the Gifts of the Spirit.

The Gifts of the Spirit should flow out of intimacy with the Lord; however, that isn't always the case:

"So then, does He who provides you with the Spirit and works miracles among you, do it by the works of the Law, or by hearing with faith??" Galatians 3:5

According to this verse, God works miracles because of faith, not good behavior or perfect character. This is why it's possible for a ministry to move in radical signs and wonders, and later found to be in compromise. Many have fallen away from the faith because of these testimonies, or attribute every miracle, word of knowledge, or prophecy to the devil because a minister wasn't walking in righteousness. The truth is, the gifts aren't to make us look good, the gifts are for the people receiving the ministry.

The stories of people who have been hurt by the inappropriate use of the gifts are many. For this reason, many churches and ministries have developed guidelines and ministry protocols. It's important to abide by these protocols to keep the person receiving prophetic ministry safe, as well as the person giving the prophetic ministry. If the person giving a word feels God sharing something with them that is against protocol, this is the moment the word is to be submitted to the leadership of the church. These are the people who would possibly know the person's situation, and can help provide wise counsel.

In the Old Testament, the prophet was the voice of God to the people. They were also the judges of the land. Sadly, many haven't understood that we are no longer in the Old Covenant where only one man or woman hears from God. We are in the New Covenant, where the Spirit of God lives in each one of us.

Let me illustrate God's desire for all people to hear His voice in the Old Testament:

"But two men had remained in the camp; the name of one was Eldad and the name of the other Medad. And the Spirit rested upon them (now they were among those who had been registered, but had not gone out to the tent), and they prophesied in the camp. So a young man ran and told Moses and said, "Eldad and Medad are prophesying in the camp." Then Joshua the son of Nun, the attendant of Moses from his youth, said, "Moses, my lord, restrain them." But Moses said to him, "Are you jealous for my sake? Would that all the Lord's people were prophets, that the Lord would put His Spirit upon them!" Numbers 11:26-29

Listen to the Father's heart through Moses, "Would that all the Lord's people were prophets, that the Lord would put His Spirit upon them!"

This sure sounds a lot like Joel 2 were it says,

"It will come about after this that I will pour out My Spirit on all mankind; and your sons and daughters will prophesy, your old men will dream dreams, your young men will see visions. Even on the male and female servants I will pour out My Spirit in those days." Joel 2:28-29

The apostle Peter quotes this verse in Acts 2 during the outpouring of the Holy Spirit. The truth is, God's Spirit has been poured out and His sons and daughter can prophesy.

"For you can all prophesy one by one, so that all may learn and all may be exhorted." 1 Corinthians 14:31

To truly prophesy is to hear God's voice. This is why above all gifts, Paul tells us to desire to prophesy. (1 Cor 14:1)

"Surely the Lord God does nothing unless He reveals His secret counsel to His servants the prophets." Amos 3:7

God only shared His secrets with the prophets in the Old Testament, but in the New Testament, God declares His secrets are shared with His friends.

Discerning of Spirits (Eyes of God)

The Discerning of Spirits is one of the most needed, as well as misunderstood, gifts in the body of Christ. When people hear the word discernment, they usually think of discerning demons in the room. Discerning demonic spirits is a part of the gift, but thankfully not the only part. Individuals with this gift can see, sense, smell, taste or even touch in the realm of the spirit.

In the spirit we have five senses, the same way we have five senses in the natural. As born again believers this is true for all of us. We all have this ability, because the Spirit of God lives in us, to discern between good and evil. There are different levels of the gifting of discerning of spirits, just as with the gifting of prophecy. All can discern, but some are especially gifted and will experience discernment more frequently; however, we can train our senses to discern good and evil.

"But solid food is for the mature, who because of practice have their senses trained to discern good and evil." Hebrews 5:14

In the Spirit we have eyes to see

Ephesians 1:18 speaks of the eyes of our heart. I have personally seen demonic spirits with my own eyes. This will often happen when the Lord is showing what might be trying to oppose someone's life, or oppose the church I am ministering in. On one occasion, I was caught up in the Spirit and saw in a vision of a demonic spirit perched like a bird in the spirit realm. I watched as the assignment of this demonic spirit was to spit darts that ended up hitting the backs of believers. In return the believers would spit darts in the back of their brothers and sisters. Through this revelation, I was able to share the vision and lead the church into repentance for back-biting and gossip, and it brought break through.

In the Spirit, we have ears to hear the voice of God

Revelation 2:29 says, "He who has an ear, let him hear what the Spirit says to the churches." Since God is spirit, after we are born again, our spiritual ears are open to hear the voice of God. God can speak to the unbeliever, and He can speak audibly or any way He chooses. For those of us who are born again, our spiritual ears become like spiritual antennas that tune into the still small voice of God. As sons and daughters of God, hearing the voice of our Father becomes a part of our adoption into the family of God.

We can taste in the Spirit

Psalms 34:8, "O taste and see that the Lord is good." I have had very few experiences in discernment through taste, but I have had a few. Stories that

I have heard where others have discerned through taste have been similar to mine. In some meetings, I have experienced the taste of something foul in my mouth, almost like metal. The first time I wasn't sure what I was experiencing, but after a while I started to notice that every time I would taste this foul taste, someone would ask me to pray for them because they had cancer. Somehow the Lord allowed me, through the gift of discerning of spirits, to taste sickness. Through this discernment, I could recognize when people needed prayer for cancer during a meeting.

We can smell in the Spirit

"But thanks be to God, Who in Christ always leads us in triumph (as trophies of Christ's victory) and through us spreads and makes evident the fragrance of the knowledge of God everywhere, for we are the sweet fragrance of Christ unto God, among those who are being saved and among those who are perishing." 2 Corinthians 2:14-15 AMP

I have been in meetings where the room filled with the scent of cinnamon. I would ask the person next to me if they could smell it also, but they often couldn't. I then began to realize I was discerning something in the spirit. Different smells have come to represent different things to me, most importantly, the fragrance of the Lord. I have also smelled very putrid smells when others couldn't, and at times that has been the Lord revealing the presence of demonic or fouls spirits in the room.

A person with a gift of discerning of spirits has to be very careful to not become critical of what they see. If they are not careful, the Lord may be revealing something negative of someone or something to teach them how to pray for the individual. The problem is that if the discerning person doesn't understand the reason they are discerning a negative thing, they can then begin to improperly judge and label the individual with what the enemy is attacking them with. When God reveals something that is negative, He is calling us to pray in the opposite spirit His perfect will over that individual's life. This is where the gift of prophecy flows with the discerning of spirits. For example, in prayer the Lord may show that a spirit is attacking an individual. After praying for that individual, and binding the demonic assignment, the Lord may release a word that speaks the opposite of what the enemy was trying to bring, and this brings them hope.

Take notice that this gift is to discern spirits. The gift of discerning of spirits discerns:

1.　　　Demons
2.　　　Angels
3.　　　Human
4.　　　Holy Spirit

Discerning of Demons

"It happened that as we were going to the place of prayer, a slave-girl having a spirit of divination met us, who was bringing her masters much profit by fortune-telling. Following after Paul and us, she kept crying out, saying, "These men are bond-servants of the Most High God, who are proclaiming to you the way of salvation." She continued doing this for many days. But Paul was greatly annoyed, and turned and said to the spirit, "I command you in the name of Jesus Christ to come out of her!" And it came out at that very moment." Acts 16:16-18

This is a great example of the spirit of discernment in operation. Take notice the woman was speaking the truth, "these men are bond-servants of the Most High God, who are proclaiming to you the way of salvation." So then how did the apostle know that this woman had a demon if the words she spoke were true? The answer is through the gift of discerning of spirits.

Teaching on discerning the demonic is always tricky. I have taught this many times, and have seen people experience incredible freedom. I have witnessed people begin to understand how God reveals the strategy of the enemy, and how it gives them the direction they need to pray victory over their own life, or another person's life. I have also experienced people falsely accusing others, who they disagreed with or have had problems with, of having demons because they 'discerned' them. This is a tough one. Here's a great scripture to help give us wisdom with this problem:

"And this I pray, that your love may abound still more and more in real knowledge and all discernment, so that you may approve the things that are excellent, in order to be sincere and blameless until the day of Christ." Philippians 1:9-10

Paul prays that our love would abound in knowledge and discernment. If we feel we perceive a demonic spirit, it's critical that we choose love in how we approach the situation. I have met many wounded believer's who were falsely accused of having a Jezebel, Absalom or other spirits with names of bible characters (spirit's who are not omniscient), simply because they had strong personalities or disagreed with a leader. The gift of discerning of spirits should cause us to have mercy for a person, and lead us to our knees in intercession for them.

Discerning Angels

From the beginning of the bible to the end of the bible, we see encounters with angels. If it weren't for the angelic realm intervening, Jesus would have been murdered long before the cross.

"Now when they had gone, behold, an angel of the Lord *appeared to Joseph in a dream and said, "Get up! Take the Child and His mother and flee to Egypt, and remain there until I tell you; for Herod is going to search for the Child to destroy Him." Matthew 2:13

If Adam and Eve saw an angel before the fall, do you think they would have been freaked out or struggled with unbelief? Probably not. Today, however, if someone says they saw an angel, we either think they need to be in the mental hospital, or have had a visit from the Angel of Light himself.

We need the word in our heart, and the Spirit of truth in operation, but angelic visitations sent from Jesus happen today. In fact many Muslims are being converted to Christ through visions, dreams, angelic visitations and visitations from Christ Himself.

Some would ask, why would the Lord send angels today to deliver a message when we have the Holy Spirit? The same question could be asked of Daniel:

"Now while I was speaking and praying, and confessing my sin and the sin of my people Israel, and presenting my supplication before the Lord my God in behalf of the holy mountain of my God, while I was still speaking in prayer, then the man Gabriel, whom I had seen in the vision previously, came to me in my extreme weariness about the time of the evening offering. He gave me instruction and talked with me and said, "O Daniel, I have now come forth to give you insight with understanding. At the beginning of your supplications the command was issued, and I have come to tell you, for you are highly esteemed; so give heed to the message and gain understanding of the vision." Daniel 9:20-23

Maybe you are thinking, "Well, that's Daniel. He was important but there's no one who needs that revelation anymore." I have sadly heard this argument more than one time. This line of thinking is in line with Cessationists. This argument says we have the bible so we don't need extra revelation. There's truth to this statement:

"But even if we, or an angel from heaven, should preach to you a gospel contrary to what we have preached to you, he is to be accursed!" Galatians 1:8

There have been many occults that have started because they had a visitation of an angel of light that preached another gospel. This is why it is critical to have a deep understanding of the word, but also to share, and allow others to test the encounters that we have. Regardless of how powerful the encounter might be, if it doesn't line up with the revelation of God in scripture, then we have to learn to reject it.

Testing spirits

The scripture teaches us that angels surround us, and some of us are able to see them when the Lord permits. These individuals are called seers. Psalms 34:7 says, "The angel of the Lord encamps around those who fear Him." Then Matthew 18:10 says, "Beware that you don't look down on any of these little ones. For I tell you that in heaven their angels are always in the presence of my heavenly Father." From these verses many believe that we have angels around us as well as that each one of us have a "guardian angel".

Another insightful verse about angels is found in John 1:

"Do you believe this just because I told you I had seen you under the fig tree? You will see greater things than this." Then he said, "I tell you the truth, you will all see heaven open and the angels of God going up and down on the Son of Man, the one who is the stairway between heaven and earth." John 1:50-51

From this verse we see the angels are on the earth and ascend to heaven. It makes sense that the angels of God would ascend and descend upon Jesus the Son of Man, but what about the sons of men?

I have personally met many people that have had angelic visitations, and have seen angels. I have also had angelic visitations. In my personal experience, they don't happen every day, and the encounters I do have don't last very long. In a few seconds, a message is delivered that leaves a life long impact to the individual hearing it, as well as to those who the word is being delivered to.

One of my most significant angelic experiences took place during a youth group meeting when I was the youth pastor. I had one of the youth leaders speaking while I sat in the back, and enjoyed the message. Suddenly, an angel appeared in my face, and then within seconds disappeared. It had a wing that covered its face, and a hand reached out that had a fiery hot coal. I jumped back in my seat, not fully understanding what I had just seen. I told the young man next to me what I had seen, and he just looked at me as if I was crazy. I fell on my face and wept in the presence of the Lord. It took me a while to realize what I had seen was found in Isaiah 6. This angel covered its face with a wing as well as had a coal in it's hand. What I understood from this encounter was that I was to embrace the fire. There was no way for me to have predicted that I would enter into one of the hardest seasons of my life. The Lord began to bring to the surface everything in me that was not of Him.

"But who can endure the day of His coming? And who can stand when He appears? For He is like a refiner's fire and like fullers' soap. He will sit as a smelter and purifier of silver, and He will purify the sons of Levi and refine them like gold and silver, so that they may present to the Lord offerings in righteousness." Malachi 3:2-3

After the season was over, I was invited to speak at a conference where unbeknownst to me, the subject was Isaiah 6. The fire of God hit the place, and transformed lives. After this meeting, I began to see God's fire hit on a regular basis when I was invited to speak. The fire of God had to purify me before it could flow through me.

Discerning the Human Spirit

Of all of the ones mentioned, discerning the human spirit will be the most controversial. Can anyone really know what's in the heart of man? When Simon the sorcerer saw the apostles laying hands on people, and that they had received the Holy Spirit, he asked to purchase the gift of God. Look at Peter's response:

"But Peter said to him, "May your silver perish with you, because you thought you could obtain the gift of God with money! You have no part or portion in this matter, for your heart is not right before God. Therefore repent of this wickedness of yours, and pray the Lord that, if possible, the intention of your heart may be forgiven you. For I see that you are in the gall of bitterness and in the bondage of iniquity." Acts 8:20-23

Take notice that Peter didn't rebuke the demon but discerned what was in Peter's heart.

"But Jesus didn't trust them, because he knew all about people. No one needed to tell him about human nature, for he knew what was in each person's heart." John 2:24 NLT

We also see Jesus using the discerning of spirits when addressing Nathaniel in John:

"When Jesus saw Nathanael approaching, he said of him, "Here truly is an Israelite in whom there is no deceit." "How do you know me?" Nathanael asked." John 1:47-48

Notice Nathaniel's response, "how do you know me?" Jesus discerned what was in Nathaniel's heart, which in returned caused him to feel known by the Lord. We are often afraid of what someone would see if they looked into our heart. That's what I love about Jesus, He always has the ability to see the good that He has deposited in us.

Discerning the Holy Spirit

This is my favorite use of the gift of discerning of spirits. We often forget that the Holy Spirit is spirit. The scripture says:

"Then John gave this testimony: "I saw the Spirit come down from heaven as a dove and remain on him. And I myself did not know him, but the one who sent me to baptize with water told me, 'The man on whom you see the Spirit come down and remain is the one who will baptize with the Holy Spirit.'" John 1:32-33

It's important to note that a bird didn't fly out of heaven and land on Jesus. John saw the Spirit coming down from heaven as a dove. I believe John saw the Spirit descend in the spirit.

I love discerning what the Spirit is doing in my life, and in the lives of others. I have been in services where the Spirit of God would manifest Himself in the room with healing, or prophecy. I have learned, and I am continuing to learn, how to be sensitive to what the Spirit wants to do. This is part of the gift of discerning of Spirits. One of the best examples of someone moving in the discerning of the Holy Spirit, is in the life and ministry of Kathryn Kuhlman. One of my favorite Kathryn Kuhlman stories was of a meeting a pastor friend of mine attended. He drove a long way to see her minister, and upon arriving was very disappointed at first. He said she wasn't the greatest speaker, and she rambled on an on, until Kathryn pointed one finger in the air and declared, "He's here!" My friend told me that the atmosphere of the entire room became electrified, and over the next few hours he watched the power of God release miracles in the room. He watched with his own eyes as people were standing up out of wheelchairs, and other notable miracles.

It became known that Kathryn Kuhlman would talk on and on until she felt the presence of the Holy Spirit manifesting, then she would do whatever He lead her to do. Her ministry was one of the greatest ministries of healings in the last century.

Power Gifts (Faith, Healing and Miracles)

Gift of Faith

Love is the currency of heaven. Love energizes faith, and nothing happens in the Kingdom of God without faith. Faith accesses the invisible realm around us. In scripture, there are three types of faith: the measure of faith, the eternal virtue of faith, and the gift of faith.

The Gift of Faith, like the other gifts, is something that "comes upon us" or is manifested through us as the Spirit wills. In that sense, as believers, we have access to all of the gifts since we possess the Holy Spirit. There may be gifts that flow through us more consistently than others, but if a spirit filled believer was dropped into an indigenous tribe somewhere, because of the Holy Spirit, they would possess all that those people need for the kingdom to be expanded.

The gift of faith is one that I have experienced often. This gift is connected to a rhema word from the Lord. The word from the Lord may not be something I hear audibly; it could come as a thought, but when declared releases the substance of faith to those who need to hear it.

"So faith comes from hearing, and hearing by the word of Christ." **Romans 10:17**

One of my most memorable experiences happened during a church service in Kansas. I was on a 40 day fast because of a prophetic word I was given about entering a season of acceleration, and I was nearing the end of the fast. I felt very weak, and all I wanted to do was sleep. As I was sitting during the time of worship, I heard a thought go through my mind, "Declare that there are going to be miracles tonight". As soon as that thought left my mind, I was filled with unbelief. God's thoughts were replaced with my own thoughts, "What if I get up there and make that declaration and nothing happens?" A friend that I was ministering with, who is a seer prophet, leaned over to me and said, "Ivan, I have never seen this before. There's an angel pacing back and forth as if he is waiting for something." I asked the Lord, "What is this angel waiting for?" I instantly heard, "Earth's response to heaven's answer." The Father spoke His plan, and He wanted to release the miraculous; but heaven was waiting for a human agent to make a declaration. So I walked up to the microphone, and declared in a very quiet voice, "There are going to be miracles today." Then I sat down.

That night I witnessed a woman in a wheelchair, whom had no cartilage in her knees, stand, walk and then dance. Then as the ministry continued, I called up other people who were struggling with the same condition, and had her minister to them. Many other people were healed that night.

The rhema word I spoke, released the gift of faith as I declared it. Even though I was wrestling personally, the atmosphere of faith filled the room. Speaking God's word will always release faith to the hearer's. In this testimony, the rhema word released the gift of faith, and that released the gift of healing. All of the gifts flow together beautifully since they are all of the same Spirit.

Gift of Healing

I have seen the gift of healing flow in four primary ways:

1.   Word of faith
2.   Word of knowledge
3.   Laying on of hands
4.   Atmosphere

"But what does it say? "The word is near you, in your mouth and in your heart"—that is, the word of faith which we are preaching." Romans 10:8

In the 1940's and 50's there was a healing revival called 'The Voice of Healing'. Men like William Branham, Gordon Lindsey, A.A. Allen, Jack Coe and Oral Roberts where the catalyst to this movement. William Branham was probably the most famous of the healing evangelists during this revival. He had an extremely accurate word of knowledge gift that led to notable healings. Branham couldn't read, but God taught him to read the bible; however, because of his challenges in reading he wasn't the best teacher. So in the beginning of Branham's ministry, he would have F.F Bosworth (the author of Christ the Healer), teach morning sessions on receiving and keeping your healing. After attending a certain amount of his sessions, people would receive a card that allowed them to take part in the night service with Branham. Branham believed that people needed to hear the word of faith to believe God for their miracle.

I have attended meetings, and ministered to people after sharing God's word on healing, and people would have already received a healing without the laying on of hands. By just hearing the living word, people received their miracle. This is true also of sharing testimonies. As we have talked about in an earlier chapter, the testimony of Jesus is the Spirit of prophecy. Sharing testimonies of the sick being healed will often increase faith in hearts to believe that God heals. "If God healed them, why would He not heal me?"

The word of knowledge for healing reveals the sickness, and then releases faith to receive the healing. The word of knowledge is a great tool in personal evangelism as well. This is frequently called power evangelism. The Lord will give a word of knowledge about a person's condition, raising their faith level to be healed, and then often 'born again' after having this encounter with God.

Laying on of Hands

"They will lay hands on the sick, and they will recover." Mark 16:18

Laying on of hands is the most common way we see people healed. In the healing ministry of Oral Roberts, he would have people line up in prayer lines while he sat on a stool. People would pass in front of him, he would lay hands on them, pray the prayer of faith, and people would receive their healing.

As someone whose love language is physical touch, I love the laying on of hands. I often feel the heart of the Father for an individual I am ministering to for healing. Laying hands for healing prayer often leads to a flow of words of encouragement, and words of knowledge for the person receiving prayer.

"While the sun was setting, all those who had any who were sick with various diseases brought them to Him; and laying His hands on each one of them, He was healing them." Luke 4:40

Imagine our Lord and savior personally laying hands on all of these sick people. The value that He had for placing His hands on, and touching them, when all that He had to do was say a word and they would have been healed. I personally believe the laying on of hands has power to bring healing to the heart as well as the physical body. Those with leprosy weren't accustomed to being touched, but Jesus stretched His hands out and cleansed them.

There is a passage in 1 Timothy that tells us not to lay hands on anyone hastily, but to straighten out the context of this verse, lets look at this verse in the amplified:

"Do not hurry to lay hands on anyone ordaining and approving someone for min-

istry or an office in the church." 1 Timothy 5:22

Once, when I was newly born again, I was asked to pray for a sick person in front of a crowd of people. I was so scared because of the pressure, and I was unsure of what to say. I thought it had something to do with me, or how I prayed. I closed my eyes and said quietly, "Jesus." I instantly saw a vision of all of heaven reach out their hands toward the sick person, and at the name of Jesus, all of heaven responded. This is a good reminder that when we pray for a sick person, their healing doesn't come because of how long we prayed, or how good we prayed, but simply because of Jesus. Healing is a part of the birthright of believers. Healing is the children's bread.

So who is to blame when someone doesn't get healed? The answer to that question should be very simple, but because of bad theology the church has confused the work of the enemy for the work of the Father. Pastor Bill Johnson of Bethel Church in Redding, California says, "Jesus is perfect theology." Many look to the book of Job for answers, or the apostle Paul's experience leaving someone sick on his missionary journey. The answer is simply that sickness and disease come from the devil not God. Jesus' ministry was to destroy the works of the devil. One of the ways He accomplished this was through healing and deliverance (1 John 3:8, Acts 10:38). We have an adversary, the devil, whose job description is to steal, kill and destroy. The devil does kill people before their time. We live in a fallen world, and sometimes we die prematurely, or get sick because of the way we treat our bodies. Is there any scriptural basis for this?

"The Lord cares deeply when his loved ones die." Psalms 116:15 NLT

"Precious [and of great consequence] in the sight of the Lord is the death of His godly ones [so He watches over them]." Psalms 116:15 AMP

"Too costly in the eyes of the LORD is the death of his faithful." Psalms 116:15NAB 1970

The NAB defends this scripture by stating in the commentary:

Too costly in the eyes of the LORD: the meaning is that the death of God's faithful is grievous to God, not that God is pleased with the death. Cf Psalm 72:14. In Wisdom 3:5-6 God accepts the death of the righteous as a sacrificial burnt offering.

The reason this is so challenging is that we have been taught that God is in control. Everything that happens is the will of God. This is bad theology at best, and at worst, a doctrine that originated in the pit of hell. If God is in control, then every child that is abused is abused because it's God's will. God is sovereign, meaning all powerful, and He has chosen out of His sovereignty to partner with men. This is called free will. Sadly, we live in a fallen world at war. When we love someone, and contend for their healing, and they are not healed, it's not God we need to blame. Its true, God could heal, but there seems to me to be more involved than whether it's God's will or not. The scripture clearly shows that all who came to Jesus were healed.

We are not perfect in our faith, or perfect in our theology in healing. My position is to pray for the sick. If they are not healed today, we'll pray again tomorrow. If someone passes away after I have prayed, I will find people with that same condition and pray for them contending for that healing. I pray for as many people as I can to be healed.

Miracles

One of my favorite miracle stories, that I personally witnessed, was when my wife Erica and I were students at YWAM (Youth with a Mission) in Kona, Hawaii. Heidi Baker, a missionary in Mozambique, Africa was our guest speaker. She shared a story of God multiplying chocolate chip cookies. There was no way for her to know that my class was responsible for the snack that afternoon, and we were dishing up chocolate chip cookies. The leader knew there was no way we had enough cookies to serve everyone since the attendance easily tripled when people caught wind that Heidi would be ministering. After hearing Heidi's testimony of God multiplying cookies to reveal His goodness to the African children, my leader said that there was no way he wasn't going to multiply our cookies. So as we passed out the cookies, we just kept passing them out, and passing them out. I personally ate three cookies, and they kept passing the cookies around.

This is an example of a miracle. Biblical miracles would be the multiplying of the fishes and loaves, the parting of the red sea, money in the fish's mouth and turning water into wine. I call miracles 'showing up' and 'showing off'. Of course healings and answered prayer are considered miracles, but for the sake of sticking to biblical definitions, healings and miracles are in different categories. Some would call a healing someone growing a limb, or metal melting inside a body; however, these are more creative miracles than healings.

Using that definition of miracles, let me share a miracle story that I experienced in Tennessee. I was a guest speaker at a conference with lots of big names. I was the new young guy. On the airplane ride my wife had a word of knowledge that there would be a man with metal in his knee that God wanted to heal. No big deal for God right? After I finished my message, I began to call out words of knowledge, and people responded; however, no one was getting healed. I felt the gift of faith come upon me, and I kept pushing for healings, but still nothing was happening. Then I heard my wife's voice pop in my head, "There will be a man in the meeting tonight with metal in his knee that God wants to heal." I repeated what I heard to the congregation, and a man came up to the front. The host of the meeting and I touched the man's knee, and we could feel the metal pins with our hands. I prayed a simple prayer, and asked the man to feel his knee. He knelt all the way down touched the knee and said, "I'm healed." He had no emotion, and that made me doubt his testimony. So I touched his knee, and I realized that I couldn't feel the pins anymore. I asked the host to touch his knee, and he couldn't feel anything either. I asked the man why he wasn't showing any emotion, and he told me, "God told me before the meeting that He was going to heal me. So I knew when you called me up I would be healed."

This man had incredible faith! After he testified of being healed, a young man with a fractured wrist told himself, "If God could melt metal in that man's knee, surely he could heal my wrist." He removed his cast, shook his arm, and noticed there was no pain. He testified of being healed, and then many of the people that responded to words of knowledge previously, started to get healed. It was like watching popcorn pop.

Later that evening there was a young man who was born a deaf mute. He heard and spoke for the first time. I will never forget that night. Signs and wonders make people wonder. They build faith in God's people to believe again. When people experience God's power through healing and miracles, it causes them to begin to believe God for their broken marriages, or even their dreams that are unfulfilled.

In every encounter that I have shared, the common denominator is always the voice of God.

Lesson 9
Hearing the Voice of God

"Here I am! I stand at the door and knock. If anyone hears my voice and opens the door, I will come in and eat with that person, and they with me." Revelation 3:20

It's important to understand the culture in which this passage is taking place. We are not talking about dinner at a fast food restaurant. In Jewish families today, as well as many other cultures, meals are long family events filled with laughter and conversation. Jesus is inviting us to a feast with Him. This scripture is used often in evangelism, and it works, but the context is actually written to believers who where in Ephesus. I love teaching this passage of scripture in the context of hearing God's voice. God knocks on the door of our hearts waiting for us to respond. The question is what does the knock of God sound like?

After sharing on angelic encounters in the previous lesson, we see that it becomes easy to dismiss the fact that God speaks that way; especially if we have never experienced it before. There are times God may speak audibly, but it's very rare. Most people that I have asked, how they hear God's voice say that His voice is very subtle. This is also how I tend to experience hearing the voice of God most often. Later in the next lesson, we are going to look at the "louder" ways God speaks, such as angels, visions, dreams etc., but right now let's discuss the subtle, still, small voice of God.

Here's a story to illustrate a subtle way God has spoken to me in the past. Once while preaching in a conference in New Jersey, my ear felt very hot. I continued to preach thinking I was just hot, and kept drinking water. After I preached, a woman walked over to me and told me that she was having a hard time believing some of my God stories, but then she saw my ear burning bright red and heard the Lord speak to her, "I'm speaking through him." That was very encouraging to me. A few months later, I was speaking at a conference in Nashville, Tennessee, where a very reputable prophet had a word for me. He told me that I would be in services, and my right ear would get burning hot with the fire of God. This was to be a sign that the gift of faith had come upon me, and I was to release miracles.

There was no way for this prophet to know that I had already experienced this months prior in a meeting. I had never read any books on someone having a burning right ear that represented the gift of faith. There are no formulas to the way God speaks. I believe God speaks to each one of us in unique ways. This is the same way that every relationship has its own ways of communicating and showing love. We have all just read the fourteen ways God speaks, but what if there are more than fourteen ways? What if God can speak to us any way He chooses? The same God who never changes, also never performed one miracle the same way in the bible. This shouldn't discourage the reader, but encourage us that God desires a relationship with us; He desires to speak to us as a friend speaks to a friend.

As believers, we have to possess the revelation that God speaks to His children. The enemy will often sow seeds of unbelief by causing us to question, "Has God really spoken?" This is why it is critical to be a student of the word. The Lord's voice will not contradict His word, however not everything God speaks to us is in His word. For example, you may hear from the Lord, through a word of knowledge, to minister to someone at a local convenience store. You won't find that in the bible, but it's clear it is God's desire that we minister to people and that God sent us to minister.

God speaks! Not spoke in the past tense, but in present tense. He is speaking to His children. In Matthew 4:4 Jesus answered, "It is written: 'Man shall not live on bread alone, but on every word that comes from the mouth of God.'" Notice that this verse isn't past tense; in some translations the word is 'proceeds' out of the mouth of God and not 'proceeded'.

"To him the doorkeeper opens, and the sheep hear his voice, and he calls his own sheep by name and leads them out. When he puts forth all his own, he goes ahead of them, and the sheep follow him because they know his voice. A stranger they

simply will not follow, but will flee from him, because they do not know the voice of strangers."John 10:3-5

Jesus was using a parable to teach that He was the good shepherd, and the sheep were to listen to His voice. We are called sheep in scripture. He is the great shepherd that leads us by His still small voice. Take notice that the voice of a stranger, he will not follow. God is confident that we will be able to distinguish between His voice, and the voice of the enemy, and yet that is one of many believer's biggest fears, that they'll be deceived.

A simple study of the names of the enemy, versus the names of God, should help us determine whose voice we are hearing.

The Names of the Holy Spirit:

Provider	Edifier	Father	Teacher
Friend	Comforter	Faithful	Love
Creator	I Am	Divine Lover	Lion of Judah
Healer	Savior	Truth	Lord
Life			

Likewise, we can more clearly discern the enemy's voice if we understand his nature. Look at a few of his names below:

The Names of the Devil:

Devil	Satan	Accuser	Serpent
Adversary	Dragon	Liar	Tempter
Destroyer	Ruler of this World	Condemner	Wicked One
Thief	Ruler of Demons	Murderer	Angel of Light (Disguised as)

Revelation from God: Can convict, but it will never condemn us, or make us feel guilty.

Revelation from the Enemy: Leads to guilt, shame, condemnation and confusion.

Revelation from Self: Can be over analytic, filled with logic and reason. It brings the focus back on ourselves, and what we are able to do to figure things out, or answer our own problems. What will remain is our striving, and our own ability. If we embrace our own self revelation and act on it, pride is already knocking at the door.

What does God's voice sound like? It's important to note that God speaks the way we hear. To me God sounds like me, sometimes like my wife, and very often like the Fathers in my life. You may remember in the first book of Samuel, when the Lord called to Samuel he ran and asked Eli if he called him. This could have simply been because Samuel heard a voice, and Eli was the only one home, or the Lord sounded like Eli to Samuel.

"That the Lord called Samuel; and he said, "Here I am." Then he ran to Eli and said, "Here I am, for you called me." But he said, "I did not call, lie down again." So he went and lay down. The Lord called yet again, "Samuel!" So Samuel arose and went to Eli and said, "Here I am, for you called me." But he answered, "I did not call, my son, lie down again." 1 Samuel 3:4-6

God will often speak the way we listen. One night while I was asleep I heard my father's voice call out my name. I woke up, and my wife smiled and said." Good morning daddy." This was the announcement of my first son. This story makes me laugh when I think about it. My wife was trying to wake me up, but it took God audibly using my father's voice to wake me up. I woke up saying, "My dad just called my name. Did you hear him?" That's when she shared the news. I have actually experienced God speaking to me with the voice of someone I respect more than once.

"The boy Samuel ministered before the Lord under Eli. In those days the word of the Lord was rare; there were not many visions. One night Eli, whose eyes were becoming so weak that he could barely see, was lying down in his usual place. The lamp of God had not yet gone out, and Samuel was lying down in the house of the Lord, where the ark of God was. Then the Lord called Samuel." 1 Samuel 3:1-4

How often do we enter the Presence of the Lord with no agenda other than to minister to the Lord? In a time when the word of the Lord was rare, that's exactly what Samuel did. There are seasons in our lives when it feels like God is not speaking to us. It is in those seasons that learning to worship and rest in the Presence of the Lord, are a must.

Samuel was lying down in the house of the Lord, where the ark of God was....

Sometimes when we don't know what to pray, or when we simply want to be with Jesus, we hear His voice. As we rest in His Presence and soak in His presence, the Lord comes into that place with us. I like to put on instrumental music and lie down. I don't pray long prayers; I just speak simple phrases to the Lord, then wait and listen for His voice. Often during this time, I will see pictures in my mind (called visions), have floods of thoughts fill my mind, or have scriptures come to my heart. By spending time in the presence of the Lord, we learn to discern the ways God speaks to us.

A good reminder for me personally while ministering to people is found in Revelation 19:10, "The testimony of Jesus is the Spirit of prophecy". When we speak a word in the name of Jesus, it means that we are speaking in the nature and character of Jesus. Jesus is the savior, redeemer, comforter, healer, life giver, Father, brother, friend and so much more. Since Jesus is the redeemer, prophecy must have a redemptive element to it. Before prophesying, ask yourself if the word reflects Jesus' testimony? Does it point people to the Father in relationship?

God may warn of coming natural disasters, or bring correction to the church, but we have to remember that God even gave Jezebel time to repent. This should serve to remind us about the nature of our Father, and what his heart is toward people even in warning or correction. Our desire should always be to reveal the heart of the Father.

My desire is to see a pure prophetic stream that has a solid understanding of the ways of God toward His people in the New Covenant. There's lots of confusion around the nature of God, which is the reason there are so many contradictions with prophetic words being released in the church today. It's my hearts desire, that as we dive into a greater understanding of the nature of God, that we will rightly represent His heart to His people and the world.

In Exodus 17:6, God tells Moses to strike the rock, and water would come out of it. Moses obeyed, and the people drank. Observe the difference in Numbers 20:8, "Take the rod; and you and your brother Aaron assemble the congregation and speak to the rock before their eyes, that it may yield its water. You shall thus bring forth water for them out of the rock and let the congregation and their beasts drink."

God does not ask Moses to strike the rock this time. He instructs Him to speak to the rock. The phrase 'to speak' in the Hebrew is the word 'dabar', which means to speak the way a friend speaks to a friend. The bible teaches us that the rock in the wilderness was Christ (1Cor 10:4). Christ was only smitten once, water and blood poured out of His side, and He will never be crucified again. Now we can speak to Him as a friend speaks to a friend. Moses misrepresented God, and struck the rock again. God was not angry, but Moses was. Notice Moses' statement:

"Listen now, you rebels; shall we bring forth water for you out of this rock?" Numbers 20:10

Moses' frustration with the people came out in the way he spoke to the people. You'll also notice, he begins to take credit for what only God can do, "shall we bring forth water for you out of this rock?" This can happen to the best of us. There can be a lot of pressure in ministry, and that is why it's critical that it flows out of relationship with the Father.

In the beginning of my ministry, I suffered with the angry young prophet syndrome. The words the Lord gave me I filtered through my own anger and frustration. Let me give you a practical example of how this could manifest. The Lord may whisper to you, "Tell my people to wake up!" God's heart may be to whisper it the way you would to a small child while they are asleep in their bed, but out of frustration, you scream it as if God is angry. There is a huge difference in the way the message can be received, even though the same words have been used.

On one occasion I stood before a church, and I put them down for an hour. That night I dreamed that I was sitting on a toilet in front of the congregation. I woke up with instant understanding. I was to publicly repent before the church. The next day I told the pastor my dream and interpreted it. He gave me a huge hug and told me that he had been praying for me. He told me the elders of the church wanted to sit down with me, and rebuke me, but he told them that I was God's son and He would bring discipline. I love that story. It was humbling, but the people embraced and forgave me.

The Lord may have us give words at times that are hard, but we must have the humility and love like Daniel the prophet had when he spoke to Nebuchadnezzar. Daniel 4:19 says, "My lord, if only the dream applied to those who hate you and its interpretation to your adversaries!" In the prophetic ministry, rightly representing the God of love must be our highest aim.

Lesson 10
Ways God Speaks

There are pitfalls to hearing God's voice. One of them being the tendency to compare the way you may hear, to the way another hears the voice of God.

"Mount Sinai was wrapped in smoke because the Lord descended upon it in fire; its smoke ascended like the smoke of a furnace, and the whole mountain quaked violently. And it happened, as the blast of the ram's horn grew louder and louder, Moses spoke and God answered him with [a voice of] thunder. Exodus 19:18-19 AMP

Moses heard God's voice in the fire, the smoke and the mountain quaking. Contrast this scripture now from how Elijah heard the Lord in 1 Kings:

"So He said, "Go forth and stand on the mountain before the Lord." And behold, the Lord was passing by! And a great and strong wind was rending the mountains and breaking in pieces the rocks before the Lord; but the Lord was not in the wind. And after the wind an earthquake, but the Lord was not in the earthquake. 12 After the earthquake a fire, but the Lord was not in the fire; and after the fire a sound of a gentle blowing. 13 When Elijah heard it, he wrapped his face in his mantle and went out and stood in the entrance of the cave. And behold, a voice came to him and said, "What are you doing here, Elijah?" 1 Kings 19:11-13

When we compare these two scriptures we see that they have the exact same manifestations, but the way God spoke to Moses wasn't the way God spoke to Elijah. Moses heard God in an extremely demonstrative way, but Elijah heard only a gentle blowing of the wind. I have encountered a lot of people in my ministry who feel as though they don't hear the voice of God. After asking a few questions, it is always the same thing. They actually hear God clearly, except they hear God in their thoughts. God's voice sounds to them as if they are just thinking something. What's amazing about this is that these people think they are missing out because they don't hear God audibly. When the truth is that they are already walking in an intimacy with the Lord where He doesn't have to yell at them. He only has to whisper. The scripture declares we have the mind of Christ, and those who walk closely to Jesus know His thoughts. We have become His, and He has become ours. This is heaven's mandate!

I once had a vision where I saw angels staring at computer screens. In the vision I was able to see what they were looking at. On the screen I saw what appeared to be a brain and a heart. I then watched as the mind of Christ overlapped our minds, and His heart became ours. All of heaven's desire is that we would walk in the new heart that was prophesied in Ezekiel 36:26, and the mind of Christ in 1 Corinthians 2:16.

Can God speak through my heart if it is wicked and deceitful?

"The heart is more deceitful than all else and is desperately sick; who can understand it?" Jeremiah 17:9

In order to get an understanding of this verse we have to ask whom was the original passage speaking to?

"The sin of Judah is written down with an iron stylus..." Jeremiah 17:1

As we can see from this scripture, the original context is speaking to the sin of Judah and not the reader. Let's look at what this same prophet prophesies just chapters later:

"The day is coming," says the Lord, "when I will make a new covenant with the people of Israel and Judah. This covenant will not be like the one I made with their ancestors when I took them by the hand and brought them out of the land of Egypt. They broke that covenant, though I loved them as a husband loves his wife," says the Lord. "But this is the new covenant I will make with the people of Israel after those days," says the Lord. "I will put my instructions deep within them, and I will write them on their hearts. I will be their God, and they will be my people."

Jeremiah 31:31-33

This passage is quoted in the book of Hebrews as well. Just too really solidly understand what God thinks of our heart; let's look at one more Old Testament prophecy:

"And I will give you a new heart, and I will put a new spirit in you. I will take out your stony, stubborn heart and give you a tender, responsive heart." Ezekiel 36:26

As you can see from the above passages, our hearts of stone have been replaced with hearts of flesh. The question is, when does this happen? It happens upon receiving Christ's spirits when we are born again. God's Spirit makes our spirit into a new creation.

"As Saul turned and started to leave, God gave him a new heart, and all Samuel's signs were fulfilled that day. When Saul and his servant arrived at Gibeah, they saw a group of prophets coming toward them. Then the Spirit of God came powerfully upon Saul, and he, too, began to prophesy." 1 Samuel 10:9-10

Saul was given a new heart, the Spirit of God came upon him and he prophesied. This is one of the closest depictions of the born again experience found in the Old Testament.

But what about scriptures like Matthew 15:19?

"For out of the heart come evil thoughts, murders, adulteries, fornications, thefts, false witness, slanders." Matthew 15:19

Out of whose heart?

"For there is no good tree which produces bad fruit, nor, on the other hand, a bad tree which produces good fruit. For each tree is known by its own fruit. For men do not gather figs from thorns, nor do they pick grapes from a briar bush. The good man out of the good treasure of his heart brings forth what is good; and the evil man out of the evil treasure brings forth what is evil; for his mouth speaks from that

which fills his heart." Luke 6:43-45

The answer is, out of the heart of the wicked. Out of the good man's heart (meaning the born again man's heart) brings forth what is good. This is so important to understand. If we were to ask a believer what the desire of his heart was, they may respond, "My marriage restored," "My children safe and healthy," "Revival in my city," or maybe "Souls saved." These are the most common things that I have heard believers say when I have asked this question. As a new creation in Christ your heart is not wicked. The Lord has actually changed our heart, and His Spirit abides within us, causing us to obey. Believers who haven't received this revelation will often wrestle with hearing God's voice. Are these desires mine or are they Gods? Through understanding the Word and the nature of God, we can discern if the Spirit is putting these desires in our heart, or if the enemy is trying to deceive us.

You may have heard this passage quoted from Psalms:

"Delight yourself in the Lord; and He will give you the desires of your heart. Commit your way to the Lord, trust also in Him, and He will do it." Psalms 37:4-5

The definition of 'delight' in the Hebrew is to be happy about something, to take exquisite delight, to make merry, or to make sport of. The Latin break down of 'desire' is to request or petition. We can also see that 'de' means of, and 'sire' means father. So simply put, the desire of our hearts is 'of the Father'. How can this be possible?

Look at the progression of this verse in Psalms 37 broken down this way:

"Be happy; take exquisite delight in the Lord. He will give you the desire of your heart. Commit your ways and put your trust in Him, and He will do it."

A huge piece of the equation is found in verse 7:

"Rest in the Lord and wait patiently for Him." Psalms 37:7

Resting in the Lord, trusting in Him, waiting patiently for Him, and trusting the timing of the Lord, all sure ways of seeing the desires in our hearts fulfilled.

A teaching I found on the Internet states:

Psalm 37:4 says, "Delight thyself also in the LORD; and he shall give thee the desires of thine heart." This verse has often been interpreted to mean that the Lord will give you whatever you want and has been used to justify selfishness, greed, and even adultery. But it doesn't mean that the Lord will give you whatever you want; it means that when you are seeking the Lord, He will put His wants or desires into your heart. He will make His desires become your desires. The Lord changes your "want to."

This is what most people are taught, and I agree; however, it's even more than that. In the New Covenant, our hearts are changed; his laws are written in our hearts, and also our minds.

"For this is the covenant that I will make with the house of Israel after those days, says the Lord: I will put My laws into their minds, and I will write them on their hearts. And I will be their God, and they shall be My people." Hebrews 8:10

John Eldredge stated it this way:

"You've been far more than forgiven. God has removed your heart of stone. You've been delivered of what held you back from what you were meant to be. You've been rescued from the part of you that sabotages even your best intentions. Our heart has been circumcised to God. Your heart has been set free." (Waking the Dead)

He then goes on to remark:

"We are free to be what he meant when he meant us. You have a new life – the life of Christ. And you have a new heart. Do you know what this means? Your heart is good." (Waking the Dead)

Seers

We discussed in an earlier chapter how God can choose to speak to us through our spiritual eyes. These are called visions. There are those in the body of Christ that visions are the primary way they hear from God. These prophetic individuals are called seers in the bible.

"Formerly in Israel, if someone went to inquire of God, they would say, "Come, let us go to the seer," because the prophet of today used to be called a seer." 1 Samuel 9:9

"As for the events of King David's reign, from beginning to end, they are written in the records of Samuel the seer, the records of Nathan the prophet and the records of Gad the seer" 1 Chronicles 29:29

Take notice in the Chronicles passage that the scripture distinguishes between the prophet and the seer. Both are prophets, but the seer describes how these prophetic individuals receive revelation from the Lord.

The Hebrew definitions for 'greater insight' is in the word 'Ra'ah', which means to see, look at, inspect, perceive, or consider, and also the word 'chozeh' meaning vision or star gazer. Seers hear the voice of God through their eyes. One of my favorite passages that pull the veil back on the life of a seer is found in 2 Kings.

"Alas, my master! What shall we do?" So he answered, "Do not fear, for those who are with us are more than those who are with them." Then Elisha prayed and said, "O Lord, I pray, open his eyes that he may see." And the Lord opened the servant's eyes and he saw; and behold, the mountain was full of horses and chariots of fire all around Elisha." 2 Kings 6:15-17

I would love to retell this story the way I imagine it. I picture Elisha as an older man sitting on a rocking chair, blanket over his waist, and sipping on a cup of tea. His younger less experienced disciple looks out the window and starts pacing back and forth freaking out. Elisha calmly prays, "Lord open my servant's eyes to see what I see."

Seers see what is happening in the realm of the spirit. It is my favorite gift. Seeing in the spirit realm what the Father is doing, changes our earthly perspective to a heavenly perspective.

When we see a vision, it is important that we understand that God is bringing us into a partnership with Him. There is a partnership with man and God to see His will accomplished on the earth. Often God will show seers what His heart is so that they can release it into the earth through declaration.

Bubbling Forth

Another Hebrew word meaning 'to prophesy', that reveals how revelation can come, is the word 'naba'. Naba means to flow, spring, bubble up, pour forth, spout, or to utter. Those with a naba prophetic flow often pray in the spirit before prophesying. This is unlike a seer who has to wait in the presence of the Lord to focus their mind and heart on Jesus through worship or meditation. A seer will often have to prophesy slower as they receive a picture from the Lord, and interpret what they are seeing; whereas a naba prophecy is more of a bubbling forth.

I have operated in both the seer and the naba flow, but most frequently I function in the naba. When I prophesy, most of the time I have no word from the Lord until I start praying for an individual. This flow requires more faith in God's desire to speak to an individual, than it does the prophetic gift. Most people want God to tell them everything before they minister to the person being highlighted, but that's not the way it generally works in this kind of flow. Prophesying this way requires faith and risk. At times I feel a supernatural faith rest upon me, and people become highlighted to me. I do not generally get a specific word for them, but as I call them out and lay hands on them, I begin to get a steady stream of thoughts from the Holy Spirit. If you are unsure if you have a gift of prophecy, start off by praying for someone by laying hands on them. Scriptures and encouraging words will flow from God's heart through you to the individual receiving prayer.

Here's a brief overview of some of the ways God speaks. It's important to remember that God can speak more ways than what have been listed. God is God! He can speak any way He chooses.

This is a non-exhaustive list of some of the ways God speaks:

1. His Word

"For the word of God is living and active. Sharper than any double-edged sword, it penetrates even to dividing soul and spirit, joints and marrow; it judges the thoughts and attitudes of the heart." Hebrews 4:12 NIV

"But his delight is in the law of the LORD, and on his law he meditates day and night." Psalm 1:2 NIV

God speaks through His word. Very early in my walk with the Lord, I earnestly pursued spiritual gifts without reading the word. I read every book on the supernatural I could get my hands on. One day while doing listening prayer, I saw a vision of a field, and then I saw a pipe with water flowing through it. The water stopped flowing, and the vision tilted on its side. I asked the Lord what He was showing me, and He said, "That's you. The water of my word is not flowing in you, and you are becoming out of balance with all spirit and no word." After this experience, I pursued a deeper knowledge of the word. I had a very hard time after that with many of the teachings that I usually would never question, but didn't know why. The Lord spoke to me and said, "I want you to be a voice, and not an echo." I felt that I needed to only listen to certain teachers for a season, and only read certain books. Most of my down time was spent in personal bible study. It was during that time that the Lord began to shift my theology. The Lord himself began to change my views on certain scriptures and teachings. When this season changed, I began teaching scripture and people remarked, "I know what you taught has been in the word this whole time, but I've never seen it before." Out of this I started to become a voice.

There is nothing wrong with reading books and listening to podcasts, but this should only be a part of our spiritual diet, not the whole meal. Learning to meditate upon the word, as well as understand the context of scripture, is critical. When I am reading the word, I will choose a book of the bible to study, and read the entire book. After that, I will go back to topics that where highlighted to me. I will make sure to get a clear understanding of the context of the verse by studying the chapter before and after. Taking scripture out of its original context creates error. It's important to note that no scripture is for private interpretation. The word of God is the sure word of prophecy.

"So we have the prophetic word made more sure, to which you do well to pay attention as to a lamp shining in a dark place, until the day dawns and the morning star arises in your hearts. But know this first of all, that no prophecy of Scripture is a matter of one's own interpretation, for no prophecy was ever made by an act of human will, but men moved by the Holy Spirit spoke from God." 2 Peter 1:19-21

Meditating upon the word brings revelation, and revelation brings the manifestation. Let me explain, as we study the word, and also meditate upon the scriptures, the Holy Spirit will begin to illuminate greater understanding and personal application. I love reading the word with my best friend and author of the bible, the Holy Spirit.

2. Still Small Voice

"The LORD said, "Go out and stand on the mountain in the presence of the LORD, for the LORD is about to pass by." Then a great and powerful wind tore the mountains apart and shattered the rocks before the LORD, but the LORD was not in the wind. After the wind there was an earthquake, but the LORD was not in the earthquake. After the earthquake came a fire, but the LORD was not in the fire. And after the fire came a gentle whisper." I Kings 19:11-12 NIV

The still small voice can also come like a flood of thoughts. One way to practice hearing the still small voice of God is through journaling. Habakkuk was told to "write the vision". I have had many students in bible schools that I have taught, struggle with hearing God's voice. One common denominator was that they all had analytical personalities. They would think they heard God and then begin to question, "Was that me or was that God?"

I'm the opposite. I'm more of a creative and visual person. I could be driving in the car thinking about nothing and hear, "Son, stay home today." It wouldn't be something I was thinking about, or asking the Lord. The last time this happened to me, my boys had a special event at school that I would have missed if I hadn't stayed home, and not taken any appointments. It was important to God that I spent time with my boys.

For those who don't have my spontaneous personality, I have found that journaling your prayers to be effective. As you write down what you think God is saying to you, it begins to break down the barriers of your mind that hinder you from realizing you hear God's voice. I have witnessed grown men weep as they wrote down pages and pages of conversations between themselves and God. Journaling conversations with God can also hold us accountable to what God has said, as well as reveals when we have missed it. I would encourage all believers to journal to enhance their experience with hearing God's still small voice.

3. Dreams

"For God does speak now one way, now another though man may not perceive it. In a dream, in a vision of the night, when deep sleep falls on men as they slumber in their beds…" Job 33:14

Dreams are a very common way for believers and unbelievers to hear the Lord. The Lord will often give dreams to the unbeliever to draw them to himself. Joseph interpreted Pharaoh's dream, and we are in a season where God is raising up Joseph's and Daniel's; those who will interpret the dreams of the Pharaohs of our day.

"As for these four youths, God gave them learning and skill in all letters and wisdom; and Daniel had understanding in all visions and dreams." Daniel 1:17

How do we know if a dream is from God?

"It shall be as when a hungry man dreams that he is eating, but he wakens with his craving not satisfied; or as when a thirsty man dreams that he is drinking, but he wakens and is faint, and his thirst is not quenched. So shall the multitude of all the nations be that fight against Mount Zion." Isaiah 29:8

I am aware that I am taking this scripture out of context; however there is a gold nugget in this verse. Dreams from God often leave us hungry for an interpretation. They will often come up in random times of the day. "Ah, I just remembered that I had a dream." There are dreams that are literal, but most dreams are parabolic in nature, filled with symbols.

Many have asked the question why God would not speak clearer to us if it's so important.

"It is the glory of God to conceal a thing, but the glory of kings is to search out a thing." Proverbs 25:2

God will often hide things for us, not from us, but why? I believe it's an invitation to intimacy. There are wonderful books and resources on the meaning of symbols. Early on I felt like I needed to read them all, but I began to find that many of the symbols didn't seem to fit what I felt the Lord was speaking to me. I had friends that had the gift of dream interpretation, and even at times the interpretation didn't bear witness. Then I came across the scripture regarding Joseph in Genesis, and realized I could get the interpretation directly from the source.

"Doesn't the interpretation belong to the Lord?" Genesis 40:8

The Lord is not a formula, but He is a living God who desires relationship with His people. The best interpretation will come from the Lord directly. He may lead you to a person, or a book, but we should always go to Him first.

4. Visions.

"It will come about after this That I will pour out My Spirit on all mankind; and your sons and daughters will prophesy, your old men will dream dreams, your young men will see visions." Joel 2:28

Visions are often referred to as mental pictures. Visions can take place internally, externally, as well as with eyes open or closed. We can't make vision's happen by willing them. I have experienced visions most often times when praying for people. The word 'vision' throws people off, when learning how to hear God's voice, because they are expecting a massive television screen to open up before them. When I share with people how I see a vision, people often exhale and say, "I've had those since I was a kid." As I pray for people a picture may pop up in my mind. I have learned to pay attention to them. I will quietly ask the Holy Spirit what He is showing me. The process of receiving a word is as the picture to the right.

1) Revelation is received from God, and is received in the many different ways shown in this chapter.

2) Interpretation understands what the Revelation means. If the Lord shows you a symbolic vision or dream, ask Him for the interpretation.

3) Application is how you apply the Revelation the Lord has given you. Sometimes He might show you something about someone for the purpose of lifting him or her up in prayer, but not telling him or her, what you know. Other times, the Lord will have you share with them what He has shown you, and ask Him what to do with the Revelation.

4) Timing is critical. It's easy to see why this is important for delivering a prophetic word to both, an individual person and corporate body of believers. Giving a word at an inappropriate time can sometimes quench what

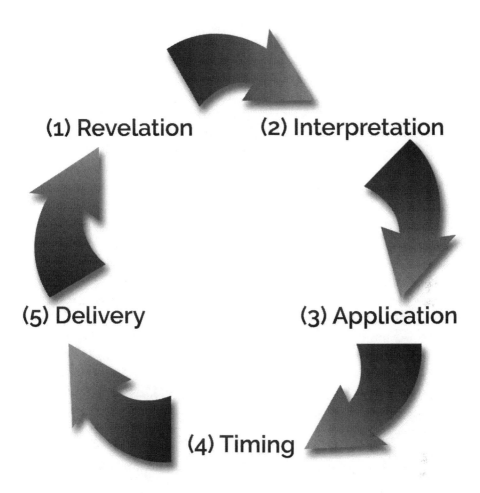

(1) Revelation

(2) Interpretation

(5) Delivery

(3) Application

(4) Timing

the Spirit is doing. However, the Lord often will open a door for a specific amount of time. This could be ten minutes, or could be a week. Simply ask God when to share what He has shown you, and be sensitive to His Spirit. If you feel you missed the open door, ask God to show you if there is another time to present the prophetic word.

5) Delivery is also very important. This is how you choose to communicate the information God has given you. You can present a word to somebody by telling them plainly, praying it over them, or writing it down and giv-

ing it to them. If it's for a corporate body of people you can sing it, pray it, dance it, or paint it. Most any form of communication can work. Ask the Lord how you should deliver what He has shown you.

Let me give you a personal experience that illustrates this point. One time during a church service the Lord gave me a picture for another guest speaker. I saw a blip on a map that kept blinking until it blipped completely off the map. I had no clue what the Lord was showing me. This would be the revelation. I then asked the Holy Spirit what He was showing me, and I had an impression that God was going to take this minister off the map. I immediately saw another picture of a minister who had a ministry to actors and actresses. Then the complete understanding came to me, like a knowing in my heart. The Lord was showing me that this individual's ministry would have a season where they would be off the map. Invitations to preach would dry up, but God would continue to provide as God rewired him to become a pastor to the stars. This word was a long shot since it didn't seem at all correct. As it turned out, years later the man went through a hard time, and he remembered the word I gave him. He now is a pastor to people in the Hollywood movie industry.

God will use our imaginations to speak to us. The new age calls this the third eye or mind's eye, but the bible calls this (in Ephesians), the eyes of our heart. Many people hear God's voice with their eyes.

"I will stand on my guard post and station myself on the rampart; and I will keep watch to see what He will speak to me, and how I may reply when I am reproved. Then the Lord answered me and said, "Record the vision and inscribe it on tablets that the one who reads it may run. For the vision is yet for the appointed time." Habakkuk 2:1-3

Notice Habakkuk said, "I will keep watch to see what He will speak to me." Habakkuk heard God's voice through a vision. We will study more about this topic later when we look at the ways God speaks.

5. Voice of the Lord

There are two ways we can hear the voice of the Lord. The inner audible voice, which many have described to sound like thunder coming from the inside, and then there is the audible voice of the Lord.

"As soon as Jesus was baptized, he went up out of the water. At that moment heaven was opened, and he saw the Spirit of God descending like a dove and lighting on him. And a voice from heaven said, "This is my Son, whom I love; with him I am well pleased." Matthew 3:16-17 NIV

I have had experiences with both the inner and audible voice of the Lord. The day I was pulled away from a bullet as an innocent bystander in a drive by shooting, I heard an inner audible voice, like a very loud thought, "Where would you go if you died right now?" I'm still amazed, and theologically confused, at how God could speak on the inside of me when I wasn't yet born again.

My encounter with the audible voice of the Lord happened months after I got born again. I loved Jesus, and felt very near to Him, but church was hard for me. I was one of the youngest guys in the church, and I went alone. I had lost all of my friends after I had gotten saved, because I stopped living the party life style. It didn't take long until I started to fall back into my old ways, and fall back into compromise. One night I was feeling tormented demonically. I had never experienced such fear. I could see something moving in my room, but it wasn't human. I curled up and wept not knowing what to do. I heard quietly in my spirit, "The blood of Jesus!" repeatedly. So I began to cry out, "The blood of Jesus! The blood of Jesus!" I began to feel a wind blow over me, and then heard audibly in my ear, "Ivan." Instantly peace came over me, and I fell asleep. When I woke up I heard my name again, but this time not in the outside of my heart, but on the inside of my heart.

The next morning when I woke up, I began to process the voice that I had heard. It was a very emotional moment for me. If my mother would have walked in my room during this moment, she would have turned the light on and asked me how I was doing because of how hard I was weeping. I knew the voice I heard wasn't the voice of my own father, because my father has a very deep voice, and I would have known if it was him. This voice was different. Then it hit me. It was God who spoke to me. This moved my heart greatly. I ran into the bathroom, and put the shower on so that my mother wouldn't hear me crying. Then a thought came into my mind, "If God spoke to me, why didn't He give me some secret message?" Then I heard as clear as day, but in my thoughts, "I'm calling you. Whenever you are ready to follow me, I'm calling you."

I know it may be hard to believe that someone has heard God's voice audibly, but it has happened to me. I knew hearing God's voice in this way didn't happened every day, but I didn't realize how uncommon it could be until I started to share my experience with other Christians. I don't believe I heard God's voice because I'm more special than anyone else, but maybe because I'm the type of guy that needs an audible voice to get my attention.

It is very interesting to me, that when I have shared the experience of hearing God's voice audibly, that many will get jealous when they hear my stories, and yet sometimes I think how funny it is that God had to yell because I wasn't listening. Some, like John, have their heads rested upon Jesus' chest, and can hear his heart beat; while others may need something more extreme to get their attention. Hearing God's voice, whether audible, or not, is still hearing the voice of God, and one experience doesn't necessarily need to be compared to the other as greater or lesser.

6. Trances

Trances are a state that God brings us into, often followed by a vision.

"I was in the city of Joppa praying, and in a trance I saw a vision. I saw something like a large sheet being let down from heaven by its four corners, and it came down to where I was." Acts 11:5 NIV

In many of Mariah Woodworth Etter's meetings in the early 1900's, trances were a very common manifestation. Young and old would fall into a trance like state, very often seeing heaven and hell. Her ministry was controversial in her day for the signs and wonders, but mostly because of the trances. One story I read was about a skeptic journalist who came to disprove the phony claims of the trance evangelist. This man personally fell into a trance, and after his experience, documented having seen heaven and hell. The experience caused him to give his life to Christ.

Trances still happen today. I haven't had many, but the one I did have took place when I was sitting in a church service listening to a sermon. I was sitting in my chair paying attention when something came over me like sleep, and I fell asleep for what felt like a second. While in this state, I saw a vision of a key chain of a number one. I have seen these types of key chains in a car dealership I had been in previously. I felt the Lord impress in my heart that there was someone in the service that was praying about starting a car dealership, and I was to confirm that it was of the Lord. I did as I felt the Lord instructed, and one gentleman responded to the word. To this day, that gentleman is still running a dealership, and uses his business primarily to help widows and single mothers who need help attaining vehicles.

7. Angels

"In speaking of the angels he says, "He makes his angels winds, his servants flames of fire." Hebrews 1:7 NIV

There are many different types of angels in the scripture, but two primary angels that are mentioned in scripture are Gabriel, a Messenger Angel and Michael (the Archangel), a Warrior Angel. The Messenger Angel brings messages, while the Warrior Angel brings protection. The job of these angels, often times, is to bring people to Christ.

"Are they not all ministering spirits, sent out to render service for the sake of those who will inherit salvation?" Hebrews 1:14

There are also beliefs that each one of us has a guardian angel.

"See that you do not despise one of these little ones, for I say to you that their angels

in heaven continually see the face of My Father who is in heaven." Matthew 18:10

Throughout this book, I share on angelic activity, but in this section I wanted to be sure to share an angelic encounter that my wife experienced. One day my wife was out running errands, and her car broke down on the side of the road. Where she broke down happened to be a very hilly area of Oregon where we lived at the time. She was forced to begin pushing the vehicle by herself up a hill. Then suddenly, from out of nowhere, a man appeared, and began pushing the vehicle for her. After the car had been pushed out of the way, she looked back to thank the man, but he was gone. This could have been a coincidence, but I didn't believe so and neither did she.

I have heard other similar stories where people have had conversations with a stranger, and the stranger says something profound that seemed to be a message from the Lord, and then appear to vanish.

"Do not neglect to show hospitality to strangers, for by this some have entertained angels without knowing it." Hebrews 13:2

Activation Exercise

What are some of the ways God has spoken to you? Ask the Lord to speak to you this month in a way He has never spoken to you before.

[Section Four]
Flowing in the Prophetic

Lesson 11
Prophetic Types

As we grow in understanding in the prophetic call, it is imperative to understand the diversity of this office. As unique as each individual's personality can be, that is how diverse the prophetic can be. No two prophets function the same way. In scripture, the word 'prophet' is attached to men like Abraham, Moses, Elijah, Elisha and Ezekiel, to name a few. Each prophet mentioned receives revelation from God differently, and then delivers the word of the Lord differently.

Abraham - The Friend of God Prophet

The first person in the bible to be called a prophet was Abraham. In Genesis 20:6-7, a heathen prince had taken Abraham's wife. God then commanded the king to restore Abraham's wife to him, saying of Abraham, "He is a prophet!" There are no recorded prophecies that Abraham declared. Abraham establishes, however, the foundation of all prophets, friendship with God.

James 2:23 says that the scripture was fulfilled when, "Abraham believed God, and it was reckoned to him as righteousness," and he was called a friend of God. Abraham's relationship with God raises the bar for all believers. His instant obedience, faithfulness and boldness to plead with God on behalf of Sodom and Gomorrah, reveals a relationship where a human has influence over God Himself.

Abraham is an example of a prophet who obeyed out of a place of trust and friendship with God. Hearing, obeying and even "wrestling" with God in prayer is an attribute we'll find in almost all of the prophets. Prophets should first be God's friends.

There are different levels of friendship:

1. Acquaintance (superficial level): This is the level where the conversation revolves around the weather or news. Nothing deep here.

2. Getting to know one another: This is where the conversation moves on to personal interest, pushing past the superficial level. In this level we discover interests and passions.

3. The Confidante: This is the level where you can entrust the secrets of your heart.

4. Covenant Friendship: This is the level of relationship God desires for His people to walk in. This level is established most often in marriage.

Friendships are built over time, through vulnerability and exposing our hearts to one another. This requires both quality time and quantity of time. The same is true with cultivating friendship with God. We give Him our hearts, we let Him see and know the deeper secrets within us, and we spend quality and quantity of time in His presence. It is out of this place we learn to recognize His voice.

In the Hebrew, the word 'shama' means both to 'hear and obey'. In the Old Testament, when God spoke to His people, the implication was that they would hear and obey. Abraham obeyed God out of faith. Obedience and friendship flow out of a heart of love for God.

"If you love Me, you will keep My commandments." John 14:15

A true prophetic person longs to have a hearing heart. So our hearts need to always be in a position to hear the Father's voice. I do this constantly when I'm talking to someone who wants counsel. I will listen with my ears, but I will also listen with my heart to hear what the Father is saying to that person.

A good example of having a hearing heart in scripture is found in the story of God appearing to Solomon. Solomon wanted to be able to have a hearing heart, to both hear God's voice, as well as to discern the heart of what the people were asking.

"In Gibeon the Lord appeared to Solomon in a dream at night; and God said, "Ask what you wish Me to give you."1 Kings 3:5

And then……

"So give Your servant an understanding heart to judge Your people to discern between good and evil. For who is able to judge this great people of Yours?" 1 Kings 3:9

This scripture displays the heart of God, and how he loves for His people to desire to hear His voice. In order to understand fully what Solomon was asking for, we have to look at it closer in the Hebrew. "Give your servant a discerning heart," said Solomon. Some translations use the phrase "hearing heart". The Hebrew word for this is 'shama', which is usually translated as a verb to 'hear', 'understand', 'listen' or 'obey'. Solomon used this word to describe his heart's desire. He didn't want to simply hear what the people said, he wanted to understand what their words implied, so he could govern wisely and "distinguish between right and wrong" (v. 9). This posture of our hearts should be true for all prophetic types.

Moses - Governmental, Signs and Wonders Prophet

"Since that time no prophet has risen in Israel like Moses, whom the Lord knew face to face, for all the signs and wonders which the Lord sent him to perform in the land of Egypt against Pharaoh, all his servants, and all his land, and for all the mighty power and for all the great terror which Moses performed in the sight of all Israel." Deuteronomy 34:10-12

The passion to hear the voice of God is found in the life of all the prophets, but how they function, and even hear the Lord, is different. Moses had one of the deepest relationships with God. His intimacy with God is more than any other prophet in scripture, other than Jesus Himself.

"Hear now My words: if there is a prophet among you, I, the Lord, shall make Myself known to him in a vision. I shall speak with him in a dream."Not so, with My servant Moses, he is faithful in all My household; with him I speak mouth to mouth, even openly, and not in dark sayings, and he beholds the form of the Lord. Why then were you not afraid to speak against My servant, against Moses?" Numbers 12:6-8

Moses didn't only have visions and dreams, he also beheld the form of the Lord. In another passage of scripture it says, "Moses spoke to God face to face" (Ex 33:11). When the scripture says 'seek God's face', the word in Hebrew is 'paneem', which is the same word for 'presence'. Moses was a lover of the Presence of God, and all forms that God spoke. As a prophetic people, hungering for God's presence should be the utmost priority of our lives.

What makes Moses different than other prophets in scripture? Well other than Elijah and Elisha, Moses is one of the few prophets that had signs and wonders following him.

What are the signs and wonders about?

"Then Moses said, "What if they will not believe me or listen to what I say? For they may say, 'The Lord has not appeared to you.'"Exodus 4:1

God then gives Moses three signs:

1. The staff became a serpent (Ex 4:2-5)
2. His hand became leprous when it went into his jacket (Ex 4:6-8)
3. Water in the Nile turned to blood (Ex 4:9)

The purpose of these signs is found in vs. 5; "that they may believe that the Lord, the God of their fathers, the God of Abraham, the God of Isaac, and the God of Jacob, has appeared to you."Exodus 4:5

Signs and wonders were understood in Moses' day as a sign that God was with the person performing them. The supernatural was commonplace in the regions of Moses' day, as was also proven by Pharaoh's magicians, as they were able to reproduce most of Moses' signs.

Moses operated in many different ways as a prophet. He not only moved in the power of God, but he also led a nation. While Moses was on Mt. Sinai for 40 days, he was shown how to build the tabernacle. He was given by God the lay out, and specific measurements of the tabernacle. Today, in the body of Christ, there are prophets that function this way. The Lord will show them the blue prints of what they are to build on the earth. Not every senior leader of a church is a five-fold pastor. Many are actually prophetic leaders, or what I call governmental prophets. Like Samuel, who found David and anointed him king, a prophetic leader can see those who have leadership on them, and place them in a position where they are functioning according to God's original design.

"Then Samuel explained to the people the behavior of royalty, and wrote it in a book and laid it up before the Lord." 1 Samuel 10:25

Prophets help to lay a foundation by seeing God's blue prints for a church, or whatever sphere they serve in. Prophetic leaders are also given structures, or what we now call 'wineskins', for movements. Some would say that this is the work of an apostle, but the blueprints are generally given to a prophet, while the apostle is the one who lays the foundation. Like Paul said, "I am a master builder." The word is 'architecron', which means 'master builder'. Samuel was a governmental prophet, and the Lord taught him the ways of royalty to pass on to kings.

Moses started off his ministry like many leaders do, meeting with every person that had need, which ultimately leads to burn out.

"It came about the next day that Moses sat to judge the people, and the people stood about Moses from the morning until the evening. Now when Moses' father-in-law saw all that he was doing for the people, he said, *"What is this thing that you are doing for the people? Why do you alone sit as judge and all the people stand about you from morning until evening?" Moses said to his father-in-law, "Because the people come to me to inquire of God. When they have a dispute, it comes to me, and I judge between a man and his neighbor and make known the statutes of God and His laws. Moses' father-in-law said to him, "The thing that you are doing is not good. You will surely wear out, both yourself and these people who are with you, for the task is too heavy for you; you cannot do it alone." Exodus 18:13-18*

God sent Jethro to give Moses a structure that would help take the burden off of him. He first told Moses to teach the people the statutes and laws, and then to make known to them the way they are to walk, and the work they are to do. He was also instructed to raise up leaders who feared God. He was to raise up men of truth, leaders of thousands, of hundreds, of fifties and of tens. Even though this scripture describes that the revelation didn't come directly from Moses, it did come from the Lord through wise counsel from Jethro. Then later, God tells Moses to pray impartation over 70 elders, that they may carry the burden. Prophetic leaders see the vision from God, and the vision reveals the people that need to be a part of the plan, as well as the structures needed to contain the wineskin.

Elijah and Elisha – The Demonstration Prophet

Elijah is known as the prophet of the Lord that moved in incredible power. In Elijah's lifetime, he was used by God to resurrected the widow's son; he called fire from heaven; he started a drought; he then prophesied and caused it to rain by the power of prayer, and that only names a few of the miracles recorded of Elijah. There are prophets today that move in signs and wonders. Elisha saw a double portion of the miracles that Elijah saw.

Demonstration Prophets are also known as Signs Prophets. They are known as such because God displays signs and wonders to confirm the prophetic word that was delivered. I have met prophets that function in this realm. One such prophet is a mentor of mine, Bobby Conner. At a meeting a friend of mine attended, he testified that Bobby was preaching about the power of God, and the need for the church to lay a hold of it. Bobby then pointed at the lights in the stadium he was preaching in, and they started to explode. Every light he pointed to exploded. This was a sign God supernaturally brought to emphasize the teaching Bobby was bringing, that the church needed to lay ahold of God's power.

The Signs Prophet are not just known by demonstration, but also the life of the prophet can be the prophetic sign. A few biblical examples of this would be the life of Hosea, and the life of Ezekiel. Hosea was told to marry a prostitute, and he named her 'Gomer' as a sign that the children of Israel were prostituting themselves with other gods. Ezekiel was told to lie on his side to bear the iniquity of the people. There are prophets today that live the prophetic word. They experience what God is going to release on the corporate body before the church will. Their lives become a parable to the body of Christ.

Samuel and Habakkuk – The Seer Prophet

"(Formerly in Israel, when a man went to inquire of God, he spoke thus: "Come, let us go to the seer"; for he who is now called a prophet was formerly called a seer.)" 1 Samuel 9:9

We have already seen, earlier in this book, the breakdown of how a seer gift functions; however, here we want to look at the function and purpose of the Seer Prophet.

I believe the call of a Seer Prophet, is to reveal the supernatural to the body of Christ. Samuel and Habakkuk are two prophets that I believe exemplify this.

Samuel had one of the most accurate word of knowledge gifts found in scripture, second to Christ. In 1 Samuel 9, by the word of knowledge, Samuel gives Saul details about his life, and what Saul was about to encounter, more than any other place found in scripture. The gifts of the seer prophet are: word of knowledge, word of wisdom and discerning of spirits. The discerning of spirits gift is the ability to see in the spirit.

Habakkuk gives insight into how the Seer Prophet's gift functions:

"I will stand my watch and set myself on the rampart, and watch to see what He will say to me, and what I will answer when I am corrected. Then the Lord answered me and said: "Write the vision and make it plain on tablets, that he may run who reads it. For the vision is yet for an appointed time; but at the end it will speak, and it will not lie. Though it tarries, wait for it; because it will surely come, it will not tarry." Habakkuk 2:1-3 (NKJV)

Take notice what Habakkuk says," I will watch to see what He will say to me." Habakkuk heard God's voice through his spiritual eyes. Seer Prophets often have visions, dreams, trances and angelic encounters. Through the sharing of the accurate revelation from God to the individuals, church, region or nation, the seer prophets reveals the closeness of heaven to us.

There are many more types of prophets we can find in scripture, as well as functioning on the earth today. This is not a comprehensive list, but a few types of prophets that have not already been mentioned that I am aware of, are as follows:

1. Writing Prophets

Rick Joyner would be a modern day writing prophet. He has seer type encounters with God that he publishes in books, and prophetic journals. Final Quest is a book by Joyner that warns, predicts and guides the body of Christ. Obviously most of the prophets in the bible wrote, or we wouldn't have their accounts. For some prophets their sphere of influence, and impact, spreads through their writing.

2. Evangelistic Prophets

These types of evangelists carry the heart of God for the lost. They are constantly prophesying of the harvest, and the need for the church to focus on the lost. Patricia King is a great example of a prophetic evangelist. She walks in the function of prophet, but one of the main focuses of her ministry is the lost.

3. Teaching Prophets

Prophetic Teachers are equippers. They love to teach and train the body to hear the voice of God, and they break up the scriptures into small chunks of bread that the people can digest. The messages they teach are messages that always carry a prophetic edge. James Goll is a great example of a prophetic teacher. He expounds on scripture like many other teachers, but carries an anointing like the Sons of Issachar, to know times and seasons. This gift allows the prophet to teach the word in a manner that brings the scripture alive to what the Father is saying in the current hour.

4. Interceding Prophet

These intercessors are carriers of God's heart for justice. They see the injustices in our land, and can literally feel God's heart breaking over them. Prophetic intercessors become God's trumpets over areas of injustice. A modern example of a prophetic intercessor would be Lou Engle. He has gathered the body of Christ in several strategic assemblies, named The Call, too fast and pray for our nation.

5. Preaching Prophet

Prophetic Preachers, different than teachers, often don't know what they are going to preach until they grab ahold of the microphone. They often start their messages by saying, "I planned a totally different message, and God changed it." These preachers become the voice of God when they are preaching. Often people will leave the message feeling like the word preached was just for them. I have experienced, in my ministry, people coming up to me after the service telling me they were upset that I used them as an example in the sermon, until they realized that I had never met them. Mike Bickle would be a modern example of a prophetic preacher.

False Prophets

"Beloved, do not believe every spirit, but test the spirits, whether they are of God; because many false prophets have gone out into the world. By this you know the Spirit of God: Every spirit that confesses that Jesus Christ has come in the flesh is of God, and every spirit that does not confess that Jesus Christ has come in the flesh is not of God. And this is the spirit of the Antichrist, which you have heard was coming, and is now already in the world." 1 John 4:1-3

Many places in scripture we are warned to beware of False Prophets. What makes a prophet a false one? I think it's important to distinguish the difference between a False Prophets, and someone who is a wrong prophet. In the New Testament, we are encouraged to practice hearing God's voice and to exercise our gifts, especially prophecy. Missing a word doesn't make the person giving the word a False Prophet.

"But the prophet who presumes to speak a word in My name, which I have not commanded him to speak, or who speaks in the name of other gods, that prophet shall die.' And if you say in your heart, 'How shall we know the word which the Lord has not spoken?'— when a prophet speaks in the name of the Lord, if the thing does not happen or come to pass, that is the thing which the Lord has not spoken; the prophet has spoken it presumptuously; you shall not be afraid of him." Deuteronomy 18:20-22

There is a lot loaded into these verses, but the first thing I want to point out is that a prophet can miss a word because they are operating out of presumption, and we are told to not be afraid of them. A False Prophet, however, is someone who is a wolf in sheep's clothing. Their prophecy is purposefully trying to steer people away from the Lord to another god. What determines a False Prophet can be broken down into these four categories:

1. Different Source.

"Beloved, do not believe every spirit, but test the spirits, whether they are of God; because many false prophets have gone out into the world." 1 John 4:1

Today there are psychics, mediums and other spiritualists that prophesy. Their source is not the Holy Spirit. This is why the scripture tells us to test the spirits.

2. Different Message.

"But even if we, or an angel from heaven, should preach to you a gospel contrary to what we have preached to you, he is to be accursed! As we have said before, so I say again now, if any man is preaching to you a gospel contrary to what you received, he is to be accursed!" Galatians 1:8-9

There are many cults in the world that seem to have a Christian foundation, but their message is not the same as the gospels.

3. Different Fruit.

"You will know them by their fruits. Grapes are not gathered from thorn bushes nor figs from thistles, are they? So every good tree bears good fruit, but the bad tree bears bad fruit. A good tree cannot produce bad fruit, nor can a bad tree produce good fruit." Matthew 7:16-18

What is the fruit of the prophet's life? Every person has clay feet, but if the prophet's life is leading people towards a path of destruction, this is a good indicator that the messenger should not be trusted.

4. Different End

"There is a way, which seems right to a man, but its end is the way of death." Proverbs 14:12

There's an old saying, "You're headed where you're going." There are many tragic stories of False Prophets forming cults that ultimately led to lives being destroyed in the end.

By reviewing the four characteristics of false prophets, we can see modern examples of False Prophets that have led false movements. Movements such as The Church of Jesus Christ of Latter Day Saints and The Jehovah's Witness. Both of these cults do not appropriately recognize the deity of Christ. Mormons believe Jesus is the brother of Satan, and Jehovah's Witnesses believe Jesus was Jehovah's first creation. These are only one of the many false teachings in these cults; however, challenging the deity of Christ is heresy.

Let's go into a brief history of both of these cults, reveal all four categories, and clearly determine False Prophets:

One significant event that gave birth to The Church of Jesus Christ of Latter Day Saints, was an angelic visitation to a man named Joseph Smith. This angel called himself Moroni, and led Joseph Smith to the golden scrolls that revealed the 'full gospel'. The scripture is clear that we are not to add to, or take away from scripture. The book of Mormon, to the Mormon Church, is as equally inspired as the bible. Another characteristic that is common among cults, is that they hold all truth. Meaning that salvation isn't through Christ alone, it's through Christ plus whatever teachings the cult decides.

Many cults believe that salvation isn't found by grace alone. Jehovah's Witnesses evangelize to secure their salvation. Jehovah's Witnesses adhere to the Bible as their sacred text, though only the New World Translation is approved for use. The movement departs from traditional Christian teaching in several key points, including a rejection of the Trinity, and a belief that Jesus is a created being.

All of this is evidence that it is important to learn to love the word of God, be a part of a healthy church community, and allow people to speak into our lives to ensure we will be kept on the straight and narrow. I have personally chosen to glean from teachers from many different streams in the body of Christ. Every facet of the body of Christ carries a truth that we all need to be strengthened. It's important that we don't begin to accuse our own brothers and sisters in Christ of being False Prophets, simply because we differ on certain doctrine. From Baptist to Pentecostal, if Jesus is Lord, then much of the doctrinal errors will work themselves out. Diversity is a beautiful thing. What is important is that we recognize what the major foundational truths are in scripture, and agree on those.

How Do I know if I'm a Prophet?

Is someone born a prophet? Can I fast and pray to become a prophet? Ultimately how do I know if I'm called to be a prophet?

I have not only heard these questions, but also personally asked these questions. I don't believe having a title is important, what is important is function. By studying the lives of prophets in scripture, you'll find that some like Jeremiah were called to be prophets when still in their mother's womb.

"Before I formed you in the womb I knew you, and before you were born I consecrated you; I have appointed you a prophet to the nations." Jeremiah 1:5

Others like Amos were called later in life.

"Then Amos replied to Amaziah, "I am not a prophet, nor am I the son of a prophet; for I am a herdsman and a grower of sycamore figs. But the Lord took me from following the flock and the Lord said to me, 'Go prophesy to My people Israel.'" Amos 7:14-15

The bottom line is, the calling of prophet is not a self-appointed one. It is one that is called by God, and recognized by people.

A great example of what I am talking about is found in the life of David. When David was just a boy, the Lord had called him to be King. God chose David, but used Samuel to anoint him King. Yet still David had to grow up in his calling, and his calling became visible to the people he was called to lead.

The scripture says of both Samuel and Jesus that they "grew in favor and stature with God and man." Someone may be called to be a prophet, but I like to picture it as a child wearing his or her parent's clothing, they still have a lot of growing to do. If Jesus had to grow in favor and stature, then to me that means that we all must grow in favor and stature.

A person called by the Lord to be prophet will have the gifts of the prophet in operation; however, this isn't the only indicator. There are many people prophetically gifted, but don't hold the ear of world leaders. Many fivefold prophets do. As we have studied earlier, there are many different types of prophets, but behind the call of a prophet is the weight of the words of God. A prophet has platform and favor given to them by God to deliver the word that the individual needs to hear. There are many modern day prophets who have ministered to Presidents and Kings. I once heard a story from a prophet about the Lord giving him, and another prophet, a word that saved a U.S President's life from an assassination.

We are all called to prophesy, as we have been learning, but we are not all called to be prophets. Prophet is a function given to the body of Christ to equip the saints to hear the voice of God, as well as to speak forth the mind and counsel of God to the people.

One practical tip that I learned from a prophet many years ago, was to journal the words the Lord gave me that He is highlighted in newspapers, the news, or on the television. This prophet would begin to intercede for certain people that the Lord highlighted, and would often times find himself bumping into that person and minister to them, or he would just mail the word. Many would follow up with him afterwards about how impacting the word was.

The Lord is raising up prophets today in every sphere of society. I have had seasons in my life where the Lord would place me in a job just to minister prophetically to the owners. In order for us to minister to high profile figures, we need to not allow any judgment in our hearts towards those individuals to be broken off of us, or the Lord will never give us the opportunity to minister to them.

More than a title, or gift, our motivation must be love. If we choose love we will never fail.

Lesson 12
Practical Keys to Flowing in Prophetic Revelation

Presence of God

"Do you not know that you are a temple of God and that the Spirit of God dwells in you?" 1 Corinthians 3:16

The revelation that the Holy Spirit abides within us will cause us to learn to listen with the ears of our hearts; turning inward to hear the voice of the Lord. Very often what I have witnessed when training people in the prophetic is that people are waiting to hear a booming voice audible in their ears; however, when they begin to learn to quiet themselves, and tune their hearts toward the indwelling of the Holy Spirit, they begin to hear clearly the whispers of God.

"The grace of the Lord Jesus Christ, and the love of God, and the fellowship of the Holy Spirit, be with you all." 2 Corinthians 13:14

Fellowship or communion with the Holy Spirit is critical in growing in intimacy with the Lord, as well as the growing ability to hear His voice. Most believers have never considered talking to the Holy Spirit, but we have to understand that He is God on the earth since the Father and Son are seated, enthroned in heaven.

Learning to enter into the Presence of the Lord, through faith and communion with the Holy Spirit, is the first key in flowing in the prophetic anointing. Let me give you an example of how this works for me. When I lay hands on someone, I make myself aware of the Presence of the Lord that abides within me. I begin to thank Him for His Presence in me, and upon me. At this point, I very often begin to discern His Presence. I begin to put my thoughts upon Him, telling the Holy Spirit how much I love Him. I then shift my prayer from worship, to asking the Holy Spirit for a word of encouragement for the person I am ministering to, and my thoughts begin to flood with pictures and words.

Rest

"Surely I have composed and quieted my soul; like a weaned child rests against his mother." Psalms 131:2

The second key is learning to rest in the Presence of the Lord. It is out of rest that revelation flows. I have often seen people who testify of not being able to hear God, but after observing the situation, I see that they are striving to hear His voice. I heard a revelation years ago, that I loved. It was the covenant name of God, Yahweh. According to Rabbinic tradition, when God spoke His name to Moses, He breathed it. I grew up with asthma, and know what it's like to struggle to breathe. As a boy, I would lose at hide and seek every time I played, because all my friends knew that all they needed to do was stay quiet for a moment, and they would hear me wheezing. Many in the church are wheezing, spiritually speaking, because they are striving so hard to please God. The scripture declares, "In Him we live and move and have our being." Life in Christ should be like breathing. It is out of this place of resting in God that revelation flows.

It is interesting to note that Adam's first day alive was the day God rested. One of Adam's first revelations of God would have been that He rested. Also in the book of Genesis, we find that the day started in the evening. So in the Hebrew culture, when the sun would set, that would be the start of a new day. Every day would be started with sleep. Rest reveals a very important aspect of the nature of God. Here's a great verse revealing this truth:

"Then Moses said to the Lord, "See, You say to me, 'Bring up this people!' But You Yourself have not let me know whom You will send with me. Moreover, You have said, 'I have known you by name, and you have also found favor in My sight.' Now therefore, I pray You, if I have found favor in Your sight, let me know Your ways

that I may know You, so that I may find favor in Your sight. Consider too, that this nation is Your people." And He said, "My presence shall go with you, and I will give you rest." Exodus 33:12-14

Moses asked the Lord two questions:

1. Who will You send with me?
2. Show me Your ways that I may know You?

The Lord responds in verse 14, "My Presence shall go with you, and I will give you rest." This revelation is found in many other places in scripture. Christ Himself declares this in Matthew:

"Are you tired? Worn out? Burned out on religion? Come to me. Get away with me and you'll recover your life. I'll show you how to take a real rest. Walk with me and work with me — watch how I do it. Learn the unforced rhythms of grace. I won't lay anything heavy or ill-fitting on you. Keep company with me and you'll learn to live freely and lightly." Matthew 11:28-30 (MSG)

Jesus is the answer to the rest we all need. He is the Lord of the Sabbath. Rest is no longer just one day off, even though that is important. Rest is found in learning to abide in Him. I do this practically by applying Philippians 4:6-9.

"Be anxious for nothing, but in everything by prayer and supplication with thanksgiving let your requests be made known to God. And the peace of God, which surpasses all comprehension, will guard your hearts and your minds in Christ Jesus. Finally, brethren, whatever is true, whatever is honorable, whatever is right, whatever is pure, whatever is lovely, whatever is of good repute, if there is any excellence and if anything worthy of praise, dwell on these things. The things you have learned and received and heard and seen in me, practice these things, and the God of peace will be with you." Philippians 4:6-9

This verse is loaded with keys, prayer and supplication with thanksgiving. This is how it all starts. I have experienced times of prayer where I left prayer more stressed than I went in. Prayer with thanksgiving shifts my emotions to the goodness of God. At this point, we begin to intentionally think or dwell on things that cause our heart to connect with the heart of God. The last verse of this Philippians scripture (v.9), is the result of this practice; the God of peace will be with you.

Compelled by Love

"For Christ's love compels us." 2 Corinthians 5:14

When the goal of our ministry is to show someone the love of God, we will never go wrong. I have missed words of knowledge in the market place before, but because my heart was to show love to the person, they were still able to encounter the Father. My faith doesn't rest on my gifting, but my faith rests on knowing God's thoughts towards His people are as numerous as the sands on the seashore. God's thoughts towards His people are filled with love. I have confidence, when ministering over people, that the Lord always has an encouraging word for His children.

Every prophetic person operates differently, but very often I will begin to feel an emotion of love connected to the word I have for the person. In that moment, God's love for them is flowing through me.

"…and hope does not disappoint, because the love of God has been poured out within our hearts through the Holy Spirit who was given to us." Romans 5:5

Faith and Risk

The fourth key is found in Galatians 5:6, "Faith works through love." Another way of saying this is, "love energizes our faith". This is one of the hardest steps, simply because stepping out in faith is taking a risk. I have met many individuals who have studied the prophetic ministry, received prayers of impartation, but have never applied the teachings. They find themselves still struggling to feel as though they have a gift of prophecy. On the other hand, I have met individuals that think, after one teaching on the prophetic, they can prophesy over everything that walks. These people may not have all the scripture, but they have the faith to apply what they have learned. A great way to step out into faith is to practice ministering to people in groups. Go out to a restaurant, and then pray quietly for the waitress. Compare notes with the others at the table, and then the bolder individual can break the ice and share what they feel the Lord showing them. Often times, after the first person cracks the ice, the rest of the group begins to feel the freedom to share.

Be Yourself

The fifth and final is key is to simply be yourself. I've been in churches where the person delivering a prophetic word first shouts out in tongues, then proceeds to speak in King James English, all the while shaking violently. This type of ministry may flow well in certain gatherings, but delivering a word like this at the office may scare a person away. Learning to be supernaturally 'natural' is a huge key in the anointing flowing without hindrance.

Study the way your gift operates. For some it's through art, song or even writing an encouraging note to someone. It's important that even though you permit the Holy Spirit to stretch your faith, that we are true to who God has called us to be. I have seen comparison shut down more people's gifts than unbelief. Learning to be comfortable in your own skin is critical to flowing at highest capacity.

Do I still get nervous when I minister to someone I don't know in the marketplace? Of course, but by using these practical keys, peace overcomes me and I yield to the Spirit of God. The reward is revealed as we see that one word from God has the potential to change someone's life. Watching people encounter God's love for the first time is one of my favorite experiences in life. God wants to use you just the way you are. Through applying these keys, the discouraged, broken and sick won't stand a chance.

[Section Five]
Supernatural Realm

Lesson 13
Open Heavens

Many in the church have been praying the prayer out of Isaiah 64, "Oh that you would rend the heavens and come down". The heart behind this prayer is beautiful. The prayer is a petition to have the manifest presence of God with us. The reality is, however, that Jesus already has rent the heavens and has come down. So much so, that the veil, in the holy of holies, was torn from top to bottom, making a place for us to have direct access to the Presence of Father God. If that's not enough, the scripture teaches us that we have been raised up with Christ and are seated with Him in heavenly places. (Eph 2:6)

The statement that, "We can have as much of God as we want." is true. Some have taught, out of the book of Deuteronomy, that the heavens are closed because of the curse, and that we are given keys to open the heavens. This is naive at best, and at worst, it is a complete misunderstanding of what Christ has accomplished for His people on the cross.

I am an open heaven! Does that sound arrogant? Well, I am a child of God, and so are you. Why is this important in a book about prophecy? When we understand the position we have in Christ, and all that He has accomplished for us, it will create a supernatural ministry out of rest with no striving.

Let's look deeper into this revelation of man being an open heaven.

In Genesis 28, Jacob had a dream that greatly impacted him:

"Then Jacob departed from Beersheba and went toward Haran. He came to a certain place and spent the night there, because the sun had set; and he took one of the stones of the place and put it under his head, and lay down in that place. He had a dream, and behold, a ladder was set on the earth with its top reaching to

heaven; and behold, the angels of God were ascending and descending on it." *Genesis 28:10-12*

"Then Jacob awoke from his sleep and said, "Surely the Lord is in this place, and I did not know it." He was afraid and said, "How awesome is this place! This is none other than the house of God, and this is the gate of heaven." Genesis 28:16-17

I have heard many teachings out of this verse that say that Jacob had an encounter because of the geographical location. This concept is what has lead to the belief that there are, what the mystics of old called, "thin places". The belief is that there are locations on the earth where there has been much prayer, and so as a result, there is more of God or access to the Spirit realm. Other teachings emphasize that the place where Jacob arrived was a place of surrender. These teachings make great messages, but in order to understand the scriptural context, we have to understand the way the Jews thought in Jacob's day.

The mindset of the people, in Jacob's day, was that their 'gods' were regional. So, for Jacob to encounter God in another region made him think, "This must be God's house." A few chapters later, Jacob realizes the full revelation at Bethel.

"Then God said to Jacob, "Arise, go up to Bethel and live there…" Genesis 35:1

And then….

"So Jacob came to Luz (that is, Bethel), which is in the land of Canaan, he and all the people who were with him. He built an altar there, and called the place El-bethel, because there God had revealed Himself to him when he fled from his brother." Genesis 35:6-7

Jacob starts with the revelation that God's house is in one geographical location, because that was where he had the dream of the heavens being open. Later when Jacob was instructed to go back to that place, he changes the name from Bethel (meaning house of God), to El Bethel (which means the God of the house of God). You see Jacob realizing, throughout his journey, that God didn't just camp out at Bethel, but was everywhere Jacob was.

Let's look at what F.B Meyer says about this verse:

"There is an open way between heaven and earth for each of us. The movement of the tide and the circulation of the blood are not more regular than the intercommunication between heaven and earth. Jacob may have thought that God was local; now he found Him to be omnipresent. Every lonely spot was His house, filled with angels. When Jacob found God in his own heart, he found Him everywhere." (F. B. Meyer, Through the Bible Day by Day).

Wow! So profound! I pray that the reader would have this same revelation. God is not far from you. Let's look at John 1 to expound being an open heaven:

"Jesus replied, "Because I said to you that I saw you under the fig tree, do you believe [in Me]? You will see greater things than this." Then He said to him, "I assure you and most solemnly say to you, you will see heaven opened and the angels of God ascending and descending on the Son of Man [the bridge between heaven and earth]." John 1:50-51 AMP

Jesus is quoting Jacob, saying that He is the fulfillment of Jacob's ladder. The only way to the Father is through the Son, and Jesus is the bridge between heaven and earth (as the amplified puts it). As children of God, we have the Spirit of God living in us the same way the angels of God ascended and descended upon Jesus. Just as Jesus is the only way to the Father, the angels ascend and descend over us because we are the gate way for people to meet Christ.

Let's look at one other scripture to solidify this point:

"Now when all the people were baptized, Jesus was also baptized, and while He was praying, heaven was opened, and the Holy Spirit descended upon Him in bodily form like a dove, and a voice came out of heaven, "You are My beloved Son,

in You I am well-pleased." Luke 3:21-22

As the heavens were opened over Jesus, they were opened over all of us. There's no place in scripture that says the heavens closed back up. We walk under an open heaven with direct access to the presence of God surrounded by angels. With this revelation, the understanding of the spiritual realm should open up to us.

Jacob had another encounter that is true for us today.

"Now as Jacob went on his way, the angels of God met him. Jacob said when he saw them, "This is God's camp." So he named that place Mahanaim." Genesis 32:1-2

Jacob had an encounter where He saw a company of angels mixed with the company of men. He called that place 'Mahanaim', which literally translates, 'the dance of two camps'. This is a picture of heaven on earth.

Understanding that heaven isn't far from us, but is actually within reach, should create confidence in our ability to hear the voice of God, and to encounter the realm where God abides.

Activation Exercise

Practice being an open heaven. Go to a public place, like a coffee shop, and quietly worship and meditate upon the word. Then begin to pray for the glory of the Lord to touch those people around you. Be open to people coming up and asking you questions about Jesus.

Lesson 14
Encountering God

The scripture declares, "All have sinned and fallen short of the glory of God". This verse has been used continually to remind God's people they are sinners saved by grace; however, the next verse is critical in understanding the full context of what was being said:

"Being justified as a gift by His grace through the redemption, which is in Christ Jesus;" Romans 3:24

Let's look at the same verse in the NLT for greater clarity:

"Yet God freely and graciously declares that we are righteous. He did this through Christ Jesus when he freed us from the penalty for our sins." Romans 3:24 NLT

Jesus took our sins upon on the cross making us the righteousness of God. The question for a Christian in the new covenant is, "Are you a sinner saved by grace, or a son being led into glory?

"For it was fitting for Him, for whom are all things, and through whom are all things, in bringing many sons to glory." Hebrews 2:10

Some may answer that both are true, but this thinking leads to dualism. This is the view that we are constantly in a fight to kill our old man, or old self. The scriptures teach that the old man has 'been' (past tense) crucified in Christ and we live by faith in the Son of God. (Gal 2:20) We are Sons and daughters who are meant to encounter our father. God is our Father, and His desire is that His sons and daughters hear His voice, as well as experience His Presence.

"[That you may really come] to know [practically, through experience for yourselves] the love of Christ, which far surpasses mere knowledge [without experience]; that

you may be filled [through all your being] unto all the fullness of God [may have the richest measure of the divine Presence, and become a body wholly filled and flooded with God Himself]!" Ephesians 3:19 AMP

Experiencing God is not only biblical, it is critical if we are to be changed into His image. We also need this experience if we are to be a vessel in which others are to encounter God.

Jesus said to the Pharisees in John 5:

"You search the Scriptures because you think they give you eternal life. But the Scriptures point to me! Yet you refuse to come to me to receive this life." John 5:39-40 NLT

The word of God should lead us to God Himself. It is God's desire that we come to truly know Him. Look at these two scriptures:

"Thus says the Lord, "Let not a wise man boast of his wisdom, and let not the mighty man boast of his might, let not a rich man boast of his riches; but let him who boasts boast of this, that he understands and knows Me, that I am the Lord who exercises lovingkindness, justice and righteousness on earth; for I delight in these things," declares the Lord." Jeremiah 9:23-24

"This is eternal life, that they may know You, the only true God, and Jesus Christ whom You have sent." John 17:3

Take notice, according to this verse, eternal life is not done by repeating a minister's salvation prayer, but is done by knowing the only true God, Jesus Christ, whom was sent. The prayer is a good start, don't get me wrong, but Lordship is what He is looking for. This is only developed through walking with God and others in discipleship.

When God chooses to reveal Himself to us, any encounters we may have through His word in worship, prayer, dream or any of the forms we have discussed, makes the word come alive. It's no longer words written on the pages of some ancient manuscript, but a word that has been written on our hearts.

Out of the encounter Moses had in Exodus 3, with a bush that burned with fire but was not consumed, he lead a nation out of slavery. Not to mention this was in a covenant with less glory than the one we are presently in.

"But if the ministry of death, in letters engraved on stones, came with glory, so that the sons of Israel could not look intently at the face of Moses because of the glory of his face, fading as it was, how will the ministry of the Spirit fail to be even more with glory?" 2 Corinthians 3:7-8

Moses had so much glory on His face that He had to wear a veil on His face. The scripture tells us that we are not to put a veil on our faces, but actually that the veil has been lifted when people turn to Christ. We are called to walk in the light of God's glory.

"Therefore having such a hope, we use great boldness in our speech, and are not like Moses, who used to put a veil over his face so that the sons of Israel would not look intently at the end of what was fading away. But their minds were hardened; for until this very day at the reading of the old covenant the same veil remains unlifted, because it is removed in Christ. But to this day whenever Moses is read, a veil lies over their heart; but whenever a person turns to the Lord, the veil is taken away. Now the Lord is the Spirit, and where the Spirit of the Lord is, there is liberty. But we all, with unveiled face, beholding as in a mirror the glory of the Lord, are being transformed into the same image from glory to glory, just as from the Lord, the Spirit." 2 Corinthians 3:12-18

We are transformed from glory to glory by the principle of beholding and becoming. When we behold the Lord in His word, we are being transformed to be like Him. It is those who have encountered God that shake cities and change nations. World changers encounter God.

"Jesus answered him, "I assure you and most solemnly say to you, unless a person is born again [reborn from above — spiritually transformed, renewed, sanctified], he

cannot [ever] see and experience the kingdom of God." John 3:3 AMP

There is a difference between entering the kingdom and seeing the kingdom. The day we take our last breath, we will enter into God's kingdom for all eternity. Seeing the kingdom means to experience God's kingdom on this side of eternity.

Then, what does the verse, "we walk by faith and not by sight", mean? Our faith in God isn't based on what we see, but faith does see. Faith sees in the realm of the spirit. A great scripture that shows that we see with the eyes of faith is found in the same story that we reviewed in an earlier lesson of Elisha and his young servant.

"Now when the attendant of the man of God had risen early and gone out, behold, an army with horses and chariots was circling the city. And his servant said to him, "Alas, my master! What shall we do?" So he answered, "Do not fear, for those who are with us are more than those who are with them." Then Elisha prayed and said, "O Lord, I pray, open his eyes that he may see." And the Lord opened the servant's eyes and he saw; and behold, the mountain was full of horses and chariots of fire all around Elisha." 2 Kings 6:15-17

In the natural, Elisha and his servant found themselves in an impossible situation. Elisha saw in the natural all the enemies, but his eyes were also open to see in the spirit that God's armies were numbered more than that of the enemies. As believers, our faith can't be based on our natural sight, but with our eyes of faith, the eyes of our spirits. We learn to see directly through the eyes of God, and as we learn to treasure God's word in our hearts, we also learn to see from heaven's perspective.

It may be hard to believe that people today are having supernatural encounters with God like those in this manual. A huge part of that is simply because we haven't been taught that, as believers, we are supernatural.

"Now may the God of peace Himself sanctify you entirely; and may your spirit and soul and body be preserved complete, without blame at the coming of our Lord

Jesus Christ." 1 Thessalonians 5:23

As new creations in Christ we are Spirit, we have a soul and live in a body. Hearing God's voice, and sensing His presence, is all taking place within our spirit man. We have lived in fallen conditions for so long, that we haven't learned to listen with our born again spirits.

The Hebrew mindset had a place for encounters with God. The culture was oratory, and they passed stories down from one generation to another. The Hebrews passed down stories of their grandfather Moses encountering God in a burning bush, or how their Great grandfather Abraham fed three men (two angels and the Lord Himself). (Gen 18:8) For a Hebrew boy growing up in the Far East, supernatural encounters were a part of their worldview. We struggle because our worldview is based more on the Greco-Roman worldview which emphasizes reason and analytical thinking. It is with the heart one believes unto righteousness, not the mind (Romans 10:10).

God has given us a brain to use it; however our brains shouldn't limit the Holy one of Israel. We don't see Adam struggling with unbelief over seeing angels or experiencing the Presence of God. This is why it's critical that we heed the words found in Romans:

"And do not be conformed to this world, but be transformed by the renewing of your mind, so that you may prove what the will of God is, that which is good and acceptable and perfect." Romans 12:2

A renewed mind isn't struggling with unbelief over miracles, healings, and angelic encounters. We are all growing in our faith, and I have personally found that people who receive the most miracles are the ones that need them the most. As we encounter God, and the breakthroughs come, the miracles become an expectation because we grow in our understanding of the ways of God. When was the last time you were in a position where you needed a word from God, or a miracle for a loved one? It's often people in these positions that have the greatest testimonies.

As New Testament believers in Christ, we are called to experience God daily. It is said in Isaiah, speaking of Jesus, that He heard His father's voice every morning.

"The Lord God has given Me the tongue of disciples, that I may know how to sustain the weary one with a word. He awakens Me morning by morning, he awakens My ear to listen as a disciple." Isaiah 50:4

Our western understanding of 'knowing' emphasizes head knowledge. This understanding hinders us from 'knowing' God the way it was understood biblically. In the Hebrew, 'knowing', is encountering, the way Joseph knew not Mary. The Hebrew word 'know' is 'yada', which means to know through experience. It is God's desire that we not only know Him intellectually but through experience as well.

While most of us long to walk with God in the garden like Adam did before the fall, the reality is that in our 'new creation reality', we have a greater reality than Adam. Adam walked with God, but God lives in us. It may take all of our years, on this side of eternity, learning to walk with God, hear His voice, bask in His presence and release His heart on the earth; but it's definitely something worth pursuing. Would you join me in the pursuit of walking with God?

Activation Exercise

Put some worship music on while reading one verse that inspires you. Pray and meditate on that verse. Then begin to posture yourself, like a sponge, and allow the word and the Spirit of God to saturate you.

Lesson 15
Walking in the Spirit

"If we live by the Spirit, let us also walk by the Spirit." Galatians 5:25

What does it mean to walk in the spirit? Does it look like asking the Lord everything? Even what we should wear?

I don't think this is what Paul is speaking about, even though some have interpreted this verse that way. Simply put, walking in the spirit is walking in love. Love fulfills the whole law. Instead of living by a set of do's and don'ts, Paul teaches us that choosing love will always lead to the right answer. There are times when the Holy Spirit will speak a very clear word that we are to prophesy, but we may not hear a voice, see a picture or have a dream. Sometimes, like Jesus, we are simply moved by compassion.

What does being moved with compassion look like? The Greek word for compassion means to be moved as to one's bowels. The expression to be moved as to ones bowels may seem weird to those of us in the 21st century, but for those in the days of Jesus, to be moved as to one's bowels, figuratively meant, to be moved by love or sympathy. Another way of saying this is to be moved by one's emotions.

For so long we have heard that we should not trust our emotions. This may be true when they are unsanctified, but can the Lord speak through our emotions? Absolutely! Jeremiah was called a weeping prophet. When the word of the Lord came upon Jeremiah, he was moved in his emotions and wept. There are times when I have walked by someone, and I felt moved with compassion (not to be confused with human sympathy). Human sympathy looks at the individual and pities them, with no supernatural cure. Being moved with godly compassion is followed up by divine intervention from the Father.

Being led by God's spirit in love doesn't always look like healing, signs, and wonders. Sometimes it looks like being led by love to listen to someone who needs a friend. I'll never forget when I was at bible school, and I was walking in the supermarket with a friend to get some late night snacks. My friend told an elderly woman there that Jesus loved her. I wasn't prepared for her response. She stopped and said, "You mean someone loves me?" I don't remember if the woman got healed, or even if she said the sinner's prayer, but I do remember her feeling so encouraged that God loved her.

"Pursue love, yet desire earnestly spiritual gifts, but especially that you may prophesy." 1 Corinthians 14:1

Engraved in my wedding ring are the words, pursue love. This is the purpose of my life. I may not get every prophecy right; not everyone I pray for may get healed, but my goal is that everyone I minister to, or come in contact with, feels the love of the Father. If our goal is to just save someone, we may be more interested in them repeating the sinner's prayer than actually encountering the Father. If our motive is love, however, when someone I pray for doesn't get healed, they still leave encouraged by God's desire to heal them. When people are treated with kindness and encouragement, they will encounter the Heart of Jesus.

I want to leave the reader with this final thought from the words of our Lord.

"This is My commandment, that you love one another, just as I have loved you." John 15:12

We have not only been commanded to love one another, but we are also empowered to love one another according to Romans 5:5, "the love of God has been shed abroad in our hearts by the Holy Spirit." My prayer, is that as a generation pursues love, and the gifts of the Holy Spirit, that the nature of Christ will flow through us, bringing a nation to the embrace of a loving Father.

Declaration Prayer

Pray this prayer out loud:

Beloved Father, I want to love others the way you love me. Fill my cup to overflowing, that out of your love for me, I can love others well for your glory. In Jesus' name!

Made in the USA
Charleston, SC
17 September 2016